Companion volume to:
VESPA
An Illustrated History
by Eric Brockway

As part of our ongoing market research, we are always pleased to receive comments about our books, suggestions for new titles, or requests for catalogues. Please write to: The Editorial Director, G. T. Foulis & Company, Sparkford, Near Yeovil, Somerset, BA22 7JJ.

Lambretta INNOCENTI

An Illustrated History

Nigel Cox

Foulis

Haynes

© Nigel Cox 1996

First published in 1996

A catalogue record for this book is
available from the British Library.

ISBN 0 85429 963 7

Library of Congress catalog card no. 95–79124

G. T. Foulis & Company is an imprint of
Haynes Publishing, Sparkford, Nr. Yeovil,
Somerset, BA22 7JJ, England

Designed & typeset by G&M
Raunds, Northamptonshire
Printed in Great Britain by
J.H. Haynes & Co. Ltd.

ACKNOWLEDGEMENTS

Writing a book like this is no easy task, especially for someone like me who spends most of his time on the telephone rather than writing. Without the help of various people it would not have been written at all.

I would like to thank Dean Harvey for his help in collecting the pictures together and taking additional photographs; Mr R. E. Cox, my father, for manning the shop so that I could find the time to write; my long-suffering wife Jo, who sadly never owned a scooter and can't understand what I see in them; Stuart Lanning of *Scootering Magazine*, who lent me a photograph of my own scooter; and lastly Julie Sutherland, who spent hours transforming my handwriting into typescript. I have never used a computer or typewriter in my life and if it wasn't for Julie I would still be tapping out the words now, one letter at a time!

All the material in this book is from my own collection, and specifications and dates are correct to the best of my knowledge. Readers should bear in mind that many of the original illustrations were themselves not of modern-day quality, but they are included here, warts and all, for their unique historic interest. I would like to thank friends from all over the world, who have or have had scooters, who I have talked to and visited and who share the same interest as me – Lambrettas.

Nigel Cox
Weston Scooter Parts
Weston-super-Mare
North Somerset

FOREWORD
by Jeff McBride

Nigel Cox spent his formative years driving not a Lambretta, but a Vespa Sportique, purchased in 1967 to coincide with his sixteenth birthday. His most desired scooter, a Lambretta SX 200, was then well beyond his budget. Many years on, in 1984 an advertisement in a local newspaper caught his attention, selling an SX 200 at a more affordable price of £10. The SX was quickly purchased and soon rekindled his enthusiasm for scooters, and for one marque in particular: the Lambretta.

Soon after obtaining the SX another Lambretta, an LD 150 mark IV, was acquired and was to be the first of many restorations. To get parts for his increasing collection, Nigel would often visit old and ex-scooter dealers in the course of his job, at the time, as a travelling salesman. Often parts were purchased in bulk, along with general Lambretta memorabilia.

Before long, fellow enthusiasts were purchasing parts from Nigel. In response a scooter shop, Weston Scooter Parts, was opened in 1986 in Weston-super-Mare, repairing, restoring, tuning, and selling Lambrettas and spare parts. Before long the growing hobby and business extended his travels beyond the UK, to Italy – the birthplace of Lambretta – and, more recently, on a global scale, in search of parts, machines, and memorabilia.

In 1991 the growing collection of Lambretta scooters and spares resulted in a move to larger premises, which has enabled him to display the most complete collection of Lambrettas to be seen anywhere, the majority of which have been restored 'in-house' and range from the Model A right through to the GP 200 Electronic. Coupled to this, a wide range of memorabilia is on show, including posters, banners, dealer signs, and even inflatables, that have been collected on his travels. More recently this collection has received considerable media attention, featuring in the national press (*The Guardian*, the *Daily Mirror*, and *The Observer*), on the radio (BBC Radio 4), and on television (BBC2's *Top Gear*, BBC1's *Points West*, and HTV's *Roadrunner*).

The growth of the shop has reflected a growing interest in older scooters, especially Lambrettas. Like Nigel, many people who had wanted a Lambretta in their youth are now purchasing one, and/or collecting associated memorabilia. Weston Scooter Parts has provided a centre for the supply of Lambretta scooters and parts, not only for the UK and Europe, but for many other countries too, most notably, perhaps, Japan. Where parts are no longer available and there is sufficient demand, Nigel often looks into the feasability of getting them back into production. A recent example has been the manufacture of LI series II leg-shields, using an original press in South America!

At his shop, Nigel is frequently contacted for advice on the rebuilding and restoration of Lambrettas, especially with regard to their original specifications. It is with this in mind that he has compiled this illustrated history of the Lambretta, using his own experience, his large collection of subject literature, and the steady stream of information that flows through his shop every day, from customers and contacts alike. It contains a wealth of information on almost all the models ever made by Lambretta. It is interesting to note that some of the earliest, namely the A and B, were sold in the UK in such small quantities first time round that early books on the marque started only with the 1952 model C or the 1953 model D. Though this period is often considered to have been the heyday of the scooter, there is every likelihood that there may actually be more models A and B in the UK now than there ever were before! Coupled to this wealth of detail is a general history of Lambretta itself.

I feel this book will become an essential companion for every serious Lambretta enthusiast.

Jeff McBride

INTRODUCTION
Lambretta an Illustrated History

There have been many books written about the Lambretta, but most of them during the period when its scooters were still in production, so that they were more concerned with repairs and technical details. In this book, utilising information that has become available since then, I would instead like to show, in pictures, the full story of the Lambretta motor scooter.

It all started in Italy with a great man named Ferdinando Innocenti. At 16 years of age he started work in a laboratory whilst still keeping up with his studies. By the time he was 18 he had opened a small workshop. This was followed by a transfer to Rome, where he began experiments in the application of steel tubes.

Having had considerable success in the years that followed, Ferdinando Innocenti considered the time was ripe to start manufacturing steel tubes on a large scale, and in 1931 he transferred his activities to Milan. His activities during the next decade were crowned with many successes, until his factory was heavily damaged by bombing during the Second World War. Though most people would have been demoralised, Ferdinando's vitality and tenacity were such that he was inspired to set about reconstruction work with renewed vigour. His intention was to provide work for 6,000 unemployed workers and to bring the company back up to its pre-war production level, at the same time adding a motoring side to the traditional engineering division.

Covering 15 million square metres, the rebuilt plant was the largest industrial complex in Milan, and had the most modern machinery. Ferdinando's son Luigi joined the company in 1947 after graduating in engineering, starting work as an ordinary technician. He was soon promoted and in 1958 was made vice-president of the Innocenti Corporation. In June 1966 Ferdinando Innocenti died, and Luigi became president of the board on 1 December. He carried on his father's great work, achieving annual sales of $160 million whilst at the same time demonstrating a whole-hearted commitment to the social welfare of the company's staff. The factory area, for instance, included many facilities for Innocenti employees, including a football pitch, basketball and tennis courts, a swimming pool, a large canteen which served 5,000 meals every day, and a complete medical centre for employees and their families.

Following the Second World War, Italy, like many other countries, found itself sorely in need of a cheap form of transport to get people back to work. Innocenti, utilising its manpower and vast range of machinery to meet this demand, designed a little scooter which it called the 'Lambretta', named after the Lambrate area of Milan. The Lambretta came onto the market in 1947, a year after the first Vespa. It had a steel frame with tubes for the handlebars and seat mounting. It had a foot gear-change, seven-inch wheels, a 123 cc engine, and it came in six colours. It was an immediate success with the Italian people.

Though many companies had built scooters before the Second World War none had ever sold them in the quantities that Lambretta did. I think the concept of something that was easy to ride, that required little maintenance, and had a cheap price tag, was all that the Lambretta needed to guarantee its success, and over the following 24 years millions of Lambretta scooters and three-wheelers were produced.

After their success in Italy, Innocenti soon looked for other markets and eventually exported to almost every other country in the world, setting up factories in India, Argentina, Brazil, Congo, Spain, Colombia, Indonesia, Ceylon, Formosa, Pakistan, and Turkey.

However, whilst Lambrettas were being made in every corner of the world, all of those to be found in Britain were imported, initially, before sales had really taken off, by a firm in Aldershot. Next they were imported by Lambretta Concessionaires Ltd, established by father and son James and Peter Agg. This was in 1951, when they imported 500 C and LC models from the Milan works. To start an agency and start selling Lambrettas in 1951 was a very difficult task, as most motor cycle dealers thought that they were a gimmick. Besides, James Agg was near retiring age after a successful career in hire purchase, motor cars, and the wine industry. At this stage in his life it was a brave undertaking, but with all the qualities of a determined salesman he took up the challenge and began to call on the established dealers. It was only a

matter of time before the roads of Britain saw more and more of these little scooters, which in turn encouraged more people to take on an agency. Some wouldn't try scooters and fell by the wayside, but others foresaw the potential of this new form of transport and prospered.

By the mid-1950s the Lambretta had made a big impression with large trade stands at the Earls Court show, even showing huge posters on the hoardings leading up to it. By now many other scooter names had already disappeared, but there was no stopping Lambretta!

For James and Peter Agg to maintain this upward trend, they needed to be sure that their customers had a good after-sales back-up service. Consequently a nation-wide chain of service stations was set up. The idea was for the main dealers to hold stock of every single Lambretta part, and to have available not only the correct workshop tools and accessories but also mechanics who had gone through the Lambretta training school. This meant that wherever you were, you could be sure of obtaining genuine parts and of getting your scooter serviced by a qualified mechanic. Although people initially took some convincing, this back-up service – aimed at customers with little mechanical knowledge – soon proved highly popular.

This was a new way to market scooters: giving advice and helping people, always having what they wanted in stock, and being able to tackle any job. Before now established dealers had been largely unused to dealing with riders who didn't know one end of a scooter from the other (motor cyclists usually knew what the problem was and repaired it themselves), but as time went by they realised the potential value of all this extra servicing and repair work and set up fully-equipped service bays.

As more and more dealerships were

taken up the Aggs' policy began to pay off. Sales went from strength to strength. Lambrettas were seen everywhere in Britain, even outselling the popular Vespa which everywhere else in Europe still outsold the Lambretta. In Britain the name of Lambretta had become synonymous with scooters, so used had the trade and public become to seeing and using them. For the Aggs it was a great success story, since at the outset it had been very hard going and only their sheer will to succeed had kept them going. Though people had been slow to change from motor cycles, by 1959 the Aggs had sold over 47,000 Lambrettas. Indeed, having sold their allocation from the Milan factory they bought in the French LD Mk IV and sold them over here too, thereby adding to their success.

To keep a network of dealers happy, Lambretta Concessionaires invested considerable sums of money on advertising. A lot of point of sale material – posters, price-tickets, signs, display boards, etc – accompanied the launch of each new model. Most main agents would also have a neon sign in the window, with various enamel signs on the walls. In addition there were many advertisements in the press, from the *Daily Mirror* to specialist scooter and motor cycle magazines, so that even if you didn't own a Lambretta you would certainly have heard of one!

In this book my aim is to convey to you just how important Lambretta was in its heyday, by covering not just the company's many different models, but also the promotional material, the tools, the toys and other collectables, and the essence of the whole Lambretta movement. Some of the items illustrated you may have seen before, but many others are unique and very rare. My pleasure, after having spent so much time collecting Lambrettas and Lambretta memorabilia, has been to gather it all together and see it printed between the covers of a single book.

Nigel Cox

Above *Lord Montagu on a 1950 Lambretta B. This scooter is in his collection today, but in this picture dating to May 1961 it was out for its ten-year test. It was driven 17 miles to Southbourne at a steady 40 mph, with no problems. Later in the day it was taken to Cabery Garage, a Lambretta service agent, where it underwent various tests on brakes and steering. It was issued with a ten-year test certificate costing 10s 6d (52¹/₂p). The scooter was donated to the museum by Lambretta Concessionaires in July 1960.*

Right *Actress Jayne Mansfield sitting on a Lambretta LI 150 in Italy. She was used by Lambretta for a lot of advertising in the early 'sixties, including a gold-plated TV 175 III which was specially made for an exhibition and still exists in Italy today.*

Left *John Charles, a famous footballer in 1958, was a centre forward in the Italian league. He is seen here by an LI 150 Series I.*

Middle *Cliff Richard (or Sir Harry Webb as he is today) sitting on an LI 150 Series I. Note the lovely accessories – nudge bar, horn cover, fork covers, foot-board extensions, and lighting flashes.*

Bottom *'That's another fine mess you've gotten me into', but not for Lambretta, always ready to utilise an opportunity for good publicity: Laurel and Hardy on two Lambretta C models in 1951.*

Right *Debbie Reynolds, sitting on a 1956 150 LD after finishing filming the bouncy comedy* This Happy Feeling *in 1958. Maybe she's just happy because she's sitting on a Lambretta!*

Week ending February 22 1958

EVERY THURSDAY 4½ᵈ

Picturegoer

with Disc Parade

Meet them inside

FRANK SINATRA

DOROTHY DANDRIDGE

PAT BOONE

MICHAEL HOLLIDAY

JOHN SAXON

ELVIS PRESLEY

DIANA DORS

ALEC GUINNESS

DEBBIE REYNOLDS

Left *Even film stars found the little Lambretta useful to get around on. Here we see Howard Duff and Ida Lupino using it on location in the desert, filming an episode of the then-popular* Mr Admas and Eve *series. Notice the rear light unit, especially made for the US market, and the large Lambretta logos on the panels.*

Below *Still in America, here we see James Cagney and Shirley Jones with a 1958 150 LD. This Lambretta appeared in many shots during the making of the film* Never Steal Anything Small.

Right *Stars Rock Hudson, Gina Lollobrigida and Bobby Darin in a beautiful shot of second series LI 125s, from a film called* Come September. *This film has been shown on television many times. The plot centres around Rock Hudson and the cast riding Lambrettas around Italy: what could be better?*

Below right *This picture shows a 1959 Lambretta LI 150 Series I being presented to their Royal Highnesses Prince Rainier and Princess Grace of Monaco. Whilst giving thanks for the Lambretta they also express their admiration for the new model of the famous Italian scooter.*

Above *Here we see the Cetra Quartet, a very popular group of singers from Italy who recorded the Lambretta Twist in 1963. This picture from the front of the record sleeve shows them on an Innocenti 950 Spyder and a Lambretta TV 175 Series III. They also appeared in an advertising film to promote the scooters.*

Left *Sitting on an LI 150 Series I is the Miss World of 1959 Penelope Ann Coelen, aged 18, from Durban, South Africa.*

Above right *Miss Lambretta of Great Britain 1958 was Miss Joyce Littler of Aintree, Liverpool. She went to the Lyceum in London to collect her prize of 100 guineas and the Daily Herald Gold Cup.*

Right *A shot of the first Miss Lambretta contest held in Italy in 1951. The contestants are sitting on C and LC models.*

Miss Lambretta
Gran Bretagna

Four girls on an LD 150 Series III. They appeared along with four Lambrettas in an Austrian film called Four Girls in Wachau, *made in 1957.*

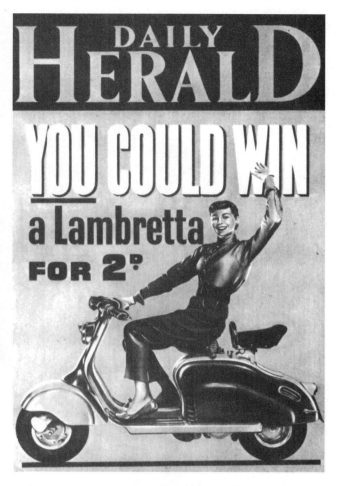

Above *This one shows Sidney Corne, a lorry driver from Tring in Hertfordshire, refusing £29 for key number nine on* Take your Pick, *a television show from the 'sixties on which he won the star prize, a red and light grey Lambretta LI 150 Series II scooter. Although he was 'gonged' in the famous 'yes/no' interlude, Sidney successfully answered three qualifying questions put to him by Michael Miles and resolutely refused to 'Take the Money' instead of opening the box. 'You've turned down £29, Sidney,' said host Michael Miles, 'and you've won tonight's star prize, the latest model of this wonderful and world famous motor scooter!'*

Above right *You could win a Lambretta LD for two old pennies in 1957. The* Daily Herald, *a very important newspaper of the time, chose a Lambretta for its top prize in a competition run by them.*

Right *If you didn't win one with* Take you Pick *or the* Daily Herald, *the Maggi Food Company ran a competition in 1963 to win 63 Lambretta scooters for consumers of its products. In the picture Lambretta importer Peter Agg (centre) speaks to Ray Gee and Louis Jan about the new poster and forthcoming competition.*

You didn't always have to buy a Lambretta – here are three shots of various competitions with Lambrettas as the star prize.

Left *David Rockefeller, president of the Chase Bank of America, visited the Lambretta works in Milan in 1957. Afterwards he tested the new TV 175 Series I.*

Below *The Lambretta motor scooter was getting more and more popular in Britain thanks to the efforts of Lambretta Concessionaires Ltd. In recognition of this Peter Agg, commercial director of Lambretta Concessionaires Ltd, was created a Knight of the Order of Merit of the Italian Republic. In this picture his knight's cross is awarded to him by the Italian ambassador in London, Count Vittorio Zoppi, during a ceremony in the London quarters of the Italian Institute for Foreign Trade in 1959.*

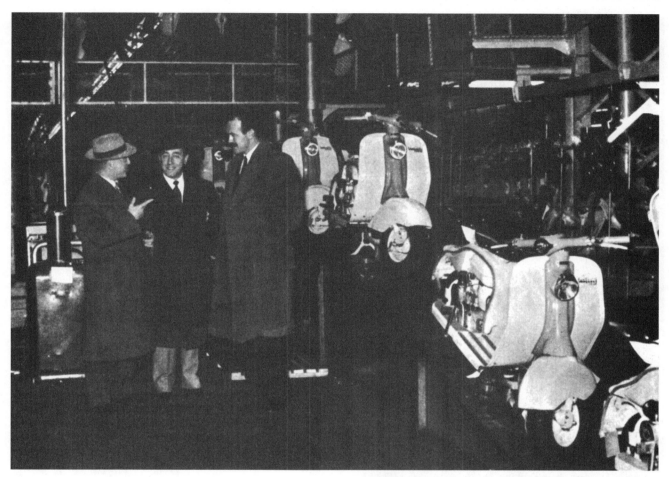

Above For years Messrs Agg – James and his son Peter, owners of Lambretta Concessionaires Ltd of London – had held the record for highest overseas Lambretta sales. They had been sole agents for Great Britain and Northern Ireland almost since the Lambretta had first appeared. Keeping pace with the new models and spares, they had created a powerful sales organization and a network of 1,000 service stations to handle after-sales service and assistance. Lambretta Concessionaires' energy had ensured that there were more Lambretta motor scooters in Great Britain than any other marque, and that no other manufacturer could match Lambretta sales. Here Peter Agg is seen talking to Ing Luigi Innocenti and Ing Giuseppe Lauro on the 150 LD production line in 1957

Right James Agg.

Above *A group of English dealers visiting the factory in Milan in 1962. Here they admire the new range of Series III Lambrettas.*

Above right *Peter Agg with some English dealers, on their way out to visit the Milan factory.*

Right *An aerial view of the factory. In the background is the famous water-tower with Innocenti written on it. This had suffered a lot of damage during the Second World War and had to be demolished, but was subsequently rebuilt to its former glory. Today the ring road round Milan is a fly-over and cuts through the middle of the factory site.*

Above *Some more shots of the factory. Rows and rows of LC and C frames are waiting to go on the overhead conveyor belts.*

Below *Another stockpile of parts, waiting to be painted before being assembled onto the finished Lambretta.*

Right *At the end of the production line, completed LD scooters and FDC three-wheelers being checked over ready for distribution all around the world. The year is 1958.*

Above left *A lorry-load of Lambretta scooters en route from Milan to Portugal. Lambrettas were spreading to all parts of the world by road, rail, air, and sea.*

Left and above *The huge press shop with 60 Innocenti medium and heavy weight presses, seen here stamping out the main backbone for the Series III Lambretta.*

Right *After they have been pressed the parts had to be stored, and this attractive circle was the way of taking up the least space. Once each layer was completed another was added on top. I estimate that there are 336 pressings in the seven layers.*

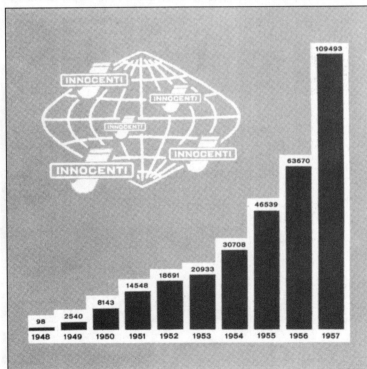

Above *A Series III gets its final check by a factory worker wearing a very desirable pair of Lambretta overalls. In the background a J model is waiting its turn.*

Left *Innocenti's success resulted from manufacturing a good-quality product and achieving high export sales. Here is a table showing the increase in foreign sales over the first ten years. In the tenth year (1957) Lambretta sales represented over 64 per cent of all Italian scooter exports.*

Above right *A display of some older Lambrettas in 1949, inside the huge Innocenti works. This was before the days of the first Lambretta club in England.*

Right *If you make lots of scooters you need to sell them! In every large city in Italy afternoon and evening newspapers compete with each other to be first into the shops. La Node, one of Italy's most important newspapers, had bought 100 Lambretta LDs for this purpose in 1958. Here we see the last batch being delivered.*

Like most important manufacturers Innocenti spent a lot of time and money creating record-breaking machines. It started right back in the early days, with model As and Bs, which were stripped down to make them lightweight. Fibreglass fairings were added and the engine and brakes modified. In England we had the normal LI 150s, but in 1962 the TV 175 III was introduced. With its disc brake and streamline design this was quite a machine, and as a result of pressure from Lambretta Concessionaires a TV 200 was specially developed for the British market, soon followed by the SX 200 and Grand Prix 200. Many of these machines were used on the race-track in England.

Above A model A racer with much modification. The barrel has a cowling to force the air through for cooling. A large carburettor has been fitted, along with larger wheels.

CLASSE 4 (sino a 125 cc.)			
1 Km. pl.	Cavanna Luigi	F. B. Mondial	130
1 Km. pf.	Cavanna Luigi	F. B. Mondial	95
5 Km.	Remondini A.	Jonghi	124
10 Km.	Remondini A.	Jonghi	119
1 Mg. pl.	Cavanna Luigi	F. B. Mondial	127
1 Mg. pf.	Cavanna Luigi	F. B. Mondial	104
5 Mg.	Remondini A.	Jonghi	125
10 Mg.	Remondini A.	Jonghi	121
50 Km.	Remondini A.	Jonghi	123
100 Km.	Remondini A.	Jonghi	123
500 Km.	Brunori-Masetti-Masserini-Rizzi LAMBRETTA		108.554
1000 Km.	Brunori-Masetti-Masserini-Rizzi LAMBRETTA		107.588
2000 Km.	Brunori-Masetti-Masserini-Rizzi LAMBRETTA		103.445
3000 Km.	Brunori-Masetti-Masserini-Rizzi LAMBRETTA		98.239
4000 Km.	Brunori-Masetti-Masserini-Rizzi LAMBRETTA		97.274
5000 Km.	Brunori-Masetti-Masserini-Rizzi LAMBRETTA		97.181
100 Miglia	Brunori-Masetti-Masserini-Rizzi LAMBRETTA		108.340
500 Miglia	Brunori-Masetti-Masserini-Rizzi LAMBRETTA		107.182
1000 Miglia	Brunori-Masetti-Masserini-Rizzi LAMBRETTA		103.507
2000 Miglia	Brunori-Masetti-Masserini-Rizzi LAMBRETTA		97.445
3000 Miglia	Brunori-Masetti-Masserini-Rizzi LAMBRETTA		97.759
1 Ora	Remondini A.	Jonghi	123
2 Ore	Brunori-Masetti-Masserini-Rizzi LAMBRETTA		108.905
3 Ore	Brunori-Masetti-Masserini-Rizzi LAMBRETTA		107.314
4 Ore	Brunori-Masetti-Masserini-Rizzi LAMBRETTA		108.304
5 Ore	Brunori-Masetti-Masserini-Rizzi LAMBRETTA		107.856
6 Ore	Brunori-Masetti-Masserini-Rizzi LAMBRETTA		107.975
7 Ore	Brunori-Masetti-Masserini-Rizzi LAMBRETTA		107.821
8 Ore	Brunori-Masetti-Masserini-Rizzi LAMBRETTA		107.346
9 Ore	Brunori-Masetti-Masserini-Rizzi LAMBRETTA		107.556
10 Ore	Brunori-Masetti-Masserini-Rizzi LAMBRETTA		104.912
11 Ore	Brunori-Masetti-Masserini-Rizzi LAMBRETTA		103.694
12 Ore	Brunori-Masetti-Masserini-Rizzi LAMBRETTA		103.863
24 Ore	Brunori-Masetti-Masserini-Rizzi LAMBRETTA		102.067
48 Ore	Brunori-Masetti-Masserini-Rizzi LAMBRETTA		97.639

Left Here is a list of records for the 125 Lambretta in 1951. In its class it was very rarely beaten, with only a Jonghi being faster in the one-hour race.

Right *A model C racer. Not all racing was about out-and-out speed. Many events, like the Isle of Man or Endurance races, took place over many hours, and many local clubs entered their own teams.*

Below *The record-breaking machine, shaped like a bullet, bright red in colour, and boasting a 125 engine. Two of these models still exist today. One, restored by Vittorio Tessera, is in the Museum of Science in Milan, while the other is in the boardroom at the Innocenti plant.*

Though everybody associates Innocenti with the production of scooters and cars, they also made a few motorbikes. In this picture is a Lambretta 250 cc twin-shaft drive, air-cooled, with lightweight wheels – all this in 1951! Really it was a warning to the motor cycle manufacturers, to show them that if they encroached too much on the scooter market, Innocenti could retaliate by producing a competitive, high-quality motor cycle of their own. Note the Series III handlebar grips.

A Lambretta go-kart. This was developed by the concessionaire for Rome, S.A.R.M.A. The engine is from the Lambro FLI 175 van, but reduced down to 125 cc to comply with racing regulations. The left-hand wheel drives directly from the engine using the original drive couplings. The frame is made of tubular steel sections and the body is fibreglass.

SOME SPECIAL PICTURES

Right *They say a dog is a man's best friend, but I'm not sure I would trust one to ride a scooter! Here we see three children and a very happy dog on a 1951 model C.*

Below The Friend of the Animals *was a weekly show on Italian television. Angelo Lombardi gives his pets – a monkey, a young bear, a lion, and a dog – a daily drive in his Lambretta FDC three-wheeler. Due to the lovely weather, in Italy a lot of Lambros didn't have doors fitted.*

Left As scooters were easy to ride a bear was trained to ride a model B around a circus ring, proving, presumably, that Lambrettas were a 'bear necessity'!

Above For the size of its engine the Lambro FLI was capable of carrying very heavy loads. This was achieved by low-gearing and heavy duty springs. In this picture a circus in America uses one to carry a real elephant.

Right It wasn't just the three-wheelers that could carry large loads. In this 1955 picture a model F supports a slightly overweight rider, who is happy to pose for the camera.

Above *In India the market for scooters has always been large, but not as large as this LD. It was built in 1953 and paraded through the streets with other, normal-sized Lambrettas.*

Left *Many things had been done with Lambrettas, but in Germany, for an April Fool's Day joke, two German-built NSU Lambrettas were joined together to form a car. The steering on the right-hand scooter is linked to the left-hand one by a rod, and fibreglass sides have been added.*

Left *Over the years, Lambretta-owners began to use their machines for more than a trip to the local shops. Here we see two Lambrettas on the Iraqi border, when things were a little safer.*

Below *On the other side of the world three American students travel from Boston to Buenos Aires in South America on 1957 LDs. Here we see them in the busy Argentinian capital.*

Right *It used to be said that Lambrettas were not reliable, but many Lambrettas of the early 'fifties travelled thousands of miles. This 1951 model C is heading for Tibet, and Innocenti were understandably quick to publicize the expedition when pictures came back.*

Lambretta

5 anno 3°
settembre · ottobre 1951
bimestrale

spedizione
in abbonamento
postale · Gruppo IV

abbonamento L. 150 · estero L. 600

Left *These two Lambrettas have done over 10,000 km on Indian roads. They have stopped for a rest in front of a mosque.*

Right *The Montin family from Australia – husband, wife, and two children – spent two years travelling to Paris by Lambretta FD three-wheeler, which also acted as their home throughout the journey.*

USES FOR LAMBRETTAS

Below *As well as scooters, cycle racing was also very popular in Italy and was regularly on national television. A TV 175 Series I was used as the pacing machine for champion cyclist Fausto Coppi when he performed a number of successful tests.*

Left *Even with a broken leg you could still ride a Lambretta. Young Antonio Sessa is seen sitting on a model B using the low front leg-shields as a support, while carrying his walking stick between them.*

Below *Many people ran businesses from their Lambrettas. Here a man in Italy has converted an FC three-wheeler, from which he sells materials, by adding an extra cupboard on the back.*

A 1957 model D with a pulley that runs from the rear wheel and, while the scooter is on its stand, drives a grinding wheel for sharpening knives and scissors. The obvious advantage of this arrangement was that you were mobile and could travel from village to village to do business.

There was always some weather protection riding a scooter, but in Italy and France back in the 'fifties many solo Lambrettas were converted into cars on two wheels. This model B has the full works, even having a windscreen wiper for really bad weather.

In the Alps around Grand San Bernard, they had plenty of snow. A man called Jean Stuper modified a Lambretta D with a track on the rear wheel and a ski on the front. This made it possible to get around in all weather conditions.

Rivalry between Lambretta and Vespa included competing to see who could get the most people on one scooter. In 1958 a team from Burgos in Spain managed to get 25 Lambrettists on a single machine, but on 21 September the same year a new record was set in Bari, in which 26 were carried. Underneath all these people is an LI 150 Series I which still managed to drive, although I suspect the ordeal didn't help its suspension!

Lambrettas were very popular in Britain, and many Lambretta clubs turned out to see the launch of the new LI at the Earls Court show in 1959. In this picture you can see the 'Innocents' Lambretta Club riding to the show. Note the huge posters on the hoardings behind, for which Lambretta Concessionaires spared no expense.

Left *In days gone by it was not only your daily pinta that was delivered to your door. There were very few supermarkets, and food and other goods were often brought in delivery vans. Here an FDC Lambro is used to sell Esso Blue paraffin on the streets of Portsmouth, with the slogan 'Delivered to your door'.*

Below *Lambretta Concessionaires were not only interested in sales, but in safety too. In 1960 they developed a twin control Lambretta using an LI 150 Series II fitted with a second pair of handlebars fitted behind the driver's seat. The throttle lever, the rear break control, and the clutch controls, besides the key for disconnecting the engine, were fitted to the second handlebar. With this arrangement an experienced rider could ride pillion to correct a learner's mistakes.*

If you were a 'True Blue Tory' the only way to prove it was to ride around London with a bowler hat and a picture of your favourite politician on your back. Of course you needed to be on an LD 150.

Lambretta Concessionaires had put a lot of thought and work into Lambrettas. Here is a sample of some of the things that went on.

Lambretta

Champion

Salesman Contest

1st OCTOBER – 30th OCTOBER 1960

1st Prize	*An Austin Seven*
2nd Prize	*A Television Set*
3rd Prize	*£25*

Left *As in any company that wanted to increase sales, it was important to motivate the staff. Many competitions were run, including this one to win an Austin Seven in 1960.*

Right *There were many aids to selling and you could order lead printing blocks from Lambretta. They would send you a list, as in the picture, from which you could choose the one you wanted. They would then send it to you free of charge, and you gave it to your local paper along with the rest of your advertisement, for which you paid in the normal way.*

Below *Another scheme was to resell used Lambrettas with a three month guarantee from Lambretta Concessionaires Ltd. This promotion was backed by advertising in the local papers and in Lambretta agents' windows.*

Lambretta take the lead again!

For the first time ever in Britain—a scheme that guarantees the condition of a used LAMBRETTA, and offers first-class safeguards to the purchaser. Lambretta scooters offered under this scheme can be purchased with complete confidence, having the full backing of Lambretta Concessionaires Limited, and their guarantee for three months.

USED SCOOTER PURCHASE MADE SAFE FOR YOU

LOOK for this sign

in your local Lambretta Agent's window. It means that he can offer you Guaranteed Used Lambrettas.

LOOK for this Guarantee Label

—one is affixed to the windscreen or legshield of *every* machine that is being offered under the Lambretta Used Scooter Guarantee Scheme.

THIS MACHINE IS GUARANTEED BY Lambretta

WHAT DOES THE SCHEME GUARANTEE?

* The machine must not have been registered for a period of longer than 24 months.
* In the opinion of the Lambretta Service Agent, the machine must not have exceeded 12,000 miles.
* The machine must have been reconditioned by an Officially Appointed Lambretta Service Agent to the high standard demanded by Lambretta Concessionaires. A broad outline of these requirements is given overleaf.

A WRITTEN Guarantee FOR 3 MONTHS

issued by Lambretta Concessionaires Limited, is given to every purchaser of a Lambretta covered by this scheme.

Keep your eye on your local papers for advertisements offering Used Lambrettas for sale . . . you can purchase one with complete confidence.

MARCH, 1957

LAMBRETTA STOCK BLOCK SHEET № 5

ALL PREVIOUS STOCK BLOCK SHEETS ARE CANCELLED AND NO BLOCKS WILL BE SUPPLIED FROM SHEETS PREVIOUS TO No. 5.

M 457 "A"
100 Screen

M 257 "A"
100 Screen

M 457 "B"
100 Screen

M 457 "C"
100 Screen

M 257 "B"
100 Screen

M 257 "C"
100 Screen

M 357 "B"
65 Screen

M 357 "C"
65 Screen

M 157 "B"
65 Screen

M 157 "C"
65 Screen

150cc MODEL | **125cc MODEL**

M 457 "D"
100 Screen

M 257 "D"
100 Screen

WHEN ORDERING PLEASE QUOTE KEY NUMBER
LAMBRETTA CONCESSIONAIRES LTD., 424-6, KINGSTON ROAD, RAYNES PARK, S.W.20
Telephone : CHErrywood 2204

There was also a considerable amount of point-of-sale material – for example, posters, calendars, mobiles, leaflets, etc, as well as price tickets on the actual scooters.

Above *Selling Lambretta scooters was one thing, but there was also all the servicing and repair work. Lambretta had a network of trained agents and it was very easy to compile a standard charge for servicing, as with new cars today. Some of the prices on this leaflet for maintaining LDs make interesting reading!*

RECOMMENDED *Maintenance Services*

500 MILES *or once monthly*

Full lubrication.
Check oil levels.
Check and adjust tyre pressures.
Clean plug and reset gap.
Adjust carburettor setting.
Check lights.
Road test and report on condition.

PRICE **10/6**
Materials and oil extra

1,500 MILES *or every 3 months*

Full lubrication.
Check levels in gear box and rear axle.
Check and adjust tyre pressures.
Clean plug and reset gap.
Adjust carburettor.
Adjust clutch.
Check brake linings and adjust shoes.
Change wheels front to rear.
Check lights.
Road test and report on condition.

PRICE **£1.1.0**
Materials and oil extra

3,000 MILES

Full lubrication.
Drain and refill oil in gear box and rear axle.
Disconnect and oil all cause controls.
Clean plug and reset gap.
Check and reset ignition.
Check lighting.
Adjust carburettor.
Adjust clutch.
Check brake linings and adjust shoes.
Change wheels front to rear.
Adjust tyre pressures.
Wash down power unit.
Check and tighten all nuts and bolts.

PRICE **£2.10.0**
Materials and oil extra

NOTE : Prices do not include lubricants, other than chassis grease and penetrating oils. Other oils and replacement parts at list prices.

Right *As Lambrettas became more popular many clubs evolved, and with them came events such as racing, rallies, shows, etc, which Lambretta Concessionaires supported. They would advertise the event and turn up with spares and technical help. As well as teaming up with BP Petrol they did quite a bit with National Petrol, together arranging events such as this one at Mallory Park in 1966.*

WELCOME TO THE **Lambretta**
HI-FLI ECONOMY TRIAL
MALLORY PARK
November 6th, 1966

Lambretta club GREAT BRITAIN

National

The British Lambretta Association was formed soon after the first Lambrettas were imported, and it arranged many social events. This pennant for a Brighton rally in 1956 would have graced an LD.

Extract from the Lambretta Leader *for Christmas 1959, 'A look at the M1 from a Lambretta': 'I was asked to be at the opening of the new M1 motor way when Mr. Marples officially declared it available to traffic this morning. By coincidence Messrs. E. Cope and Sons of Coventry had sent through an urgent message the night before asking for the immediate delivery of a spare part to satisfy a particular customer. By combining a scooter journey of experiment on the new motor way it was given to me also to make the particularly rapid delivery of the spare part required. This was no test run on an open road, but the first example of its normal use by scooter for rapid transit. I left the start of the new road at 10.30 a.m. and handed over the spare part to Messrs. Cope's service van, which was waiting for me at the Birmingham end of the motor way, at 11.45 a.m. Returning immediately after refilling with petrol I found that I had clocked exactly 142 miles easy travelling in 170 minutes including the delivery to Copes and refuelling. The new Series II Lambretta LI 150 that I was riding moved extremely easily over this 71 mile stretch and the engine could have been kept flat out all the way, but some little variations in speed are advisable both for engine and rider. Perhaps the most important lesson to be learnt in riding or driving on this new motor way will be the sorting out of traffic into its correct lanes. From this preliminary test on a Lambretta there is no doubt in my mind as to the suitability of main "motor ways" for scootering.' Brian Gibbs.*

Right *Out of the thousand-odd dealers that once existed, few survive today. Many closed down in the 'seventies when Innocenti stopped production, and the Spanish model was brought in. However, a firm called R. W. Horner's of Ayres Road, Manchester, is still going. Many scooterists will know them for that 'hard-to-get' bit and their friendly chats. The original Mr Horner started the business in 1914 with a slogan of 'attend to service and the sales look after themselves'. One by one his three sons joined the company, and in the early 'fifties they took over the Lambretta agency with a stock of three scooters and £150-worth of spares. From that day on they never looked back. Sadly Ernest has now retired but Robert and John still sell new scooters and push-bikes.*

Below *Two people look adoringly into a shop window at an LI Series II which has been cut away to reveal the workings. Lambretta made many of these cutaway machines as new models were launched, and loaned them to shops for display purposes.*

Peter Agg and the Italian Ambassador (His Excellency Count Zoppi) visiting the Lambretta stand at the 32nd Motor Cycle Show at Earls Court in 1958. They are looking at a cutaway LI Series I.

A display of Lambrettas in Padova, Italy, in the early 1950s, with B models and a rare FB three-wheeler.

A beautiful display of Lambretta LDs, with neon signs, cutaway engines, posters, and stands. When Innocenti put on an exhibition they made sure it was done properly, with no expense spared.

A row of TV 175 Series IIs outside the main dealer in Rome. These scooters are going to be used for a cycling race taking place in the surrounding area.

Above *Another display of Lambrettas, with all the scooters parked in a square for a rally in Italy in 1957.*

Left *A TV 200 with many accessories fitted. This is one of the pictures that Lambretta Concessionaires used for publicity.*

Right *Once you had bought your scooter, you needed to customize it with accessories. These were very popular, from chrome parts to plastic tassels on the handlebars, and many companies made them. Here is a Christmas advertisement from Lambretta Concessionaires detailing the presents you could buy for your loved one.*

Left *A typical 'sixties shot, two people sitting on a 'Pacemaker' with not a care in the world.*

Below *Two lovers talk behind a TV 175 Series III. This was one of a series of photographs with young people sitting looking at Lambrettas.*

Right *An LD with all the extras at the Earls Court show. In the background is an interesting number plate, LAM 56. Note that what looks like a spot light on top of the handlebars is in fact a Faras radio with a short aerial sticking up, something which is impossible to find now.*

Below right *There were many collectable items. Here are some stamps celebrating Lambretta conventions in 1963.*

Right *One of the hundreds of posters Innocenti used to print, all in beautiful colour. This one shows a couple on a J 'Starstream'.*

Below *Another poster, this time of an SX 150, showing how cool and trendy scooters were. A typical 'sixties look, with a smart suit.*

Above *In order to advertise that you were a Lambretta agent one of the things that you needed was a dealership sign. Here are some early ones in red and white. Later on they changed to blue and white. These hung outside your shop or were screwed to the wall.*

Below *All over Italy they loved their signs, and as you drove into towns there were large numbers of notice-boards advertising shops and motor agents.*

In Britain, Lambrettas were used to promote a racy new image. To have a Lambretta was to be 'with it', as you can see by this poster. In those days, people will remember, it was not necessary to wear a helmet.

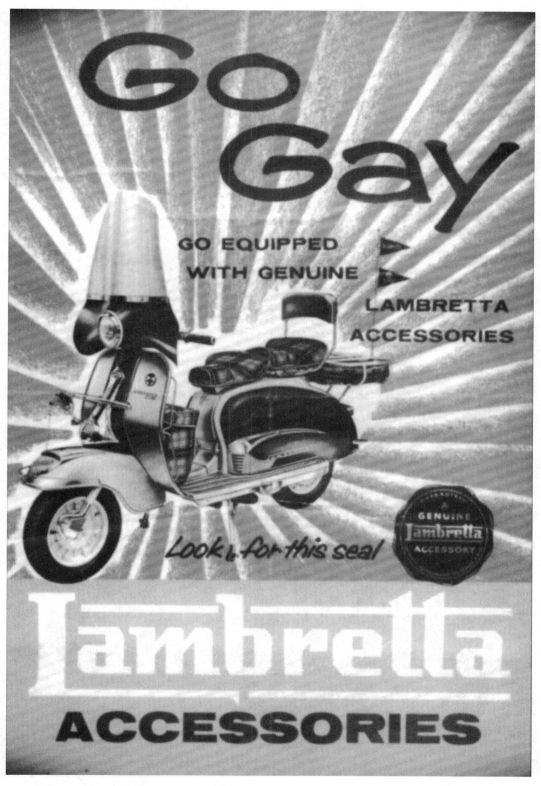

'Go gay', not a slogan that Lambrettas would have used today, but in the 1960s it meant something completely different. On this poster, promoting genuine Lambretta accessories, is an LI 150 Series II.

An early professionally painted poster from the 1950s, of a Model B, one of a few surviving originals. It has now been copied and is available to buy.

The colourful world of Lambrettas

The sun always shines on Lambrettas.

It's thirsty work riding a Lambretta.

The famous 'cowboy and dog' advertisement that introduced Lambretta to the world. It was also reproduced as a mural on the workshop of Italian restorer Vittorio Tessera.

Left *Cheesy grins welcome the new Lambretta Grand Prix or DL series in 1969. It was a quick styling job by car designer Bertone.*

Below *On the waterfront – seaside scooter rallies are nothing new.*

Right *Three wheels on my wagon – in India maybe, where three-wheelers are still a common sight.*

Lady on an LD, caught off guard at Buckingham Palace.

Linea e colore: gioia di vivere.

Line and colour: joy of living.
Ligne et couleur: joie de vivre.
Linie und Farbe: Lebensfreude.

INNOCENTI

SOC. GENERALE PER L'INDUSTRIA METALLURGICA E MECCANICA

MILANO

NEW YORK   PARIGI   ROMA   LONDRA   CARACAS

PRINTED IN ITALY

L. 100

Curvaceous models. As the 1960s progressed fashion for both women and Lambrettas called for something slimmer.

'That exhaust on your Lambretta makes a racket!'
Early 1960s Lambrettisti loved a brush with nature.

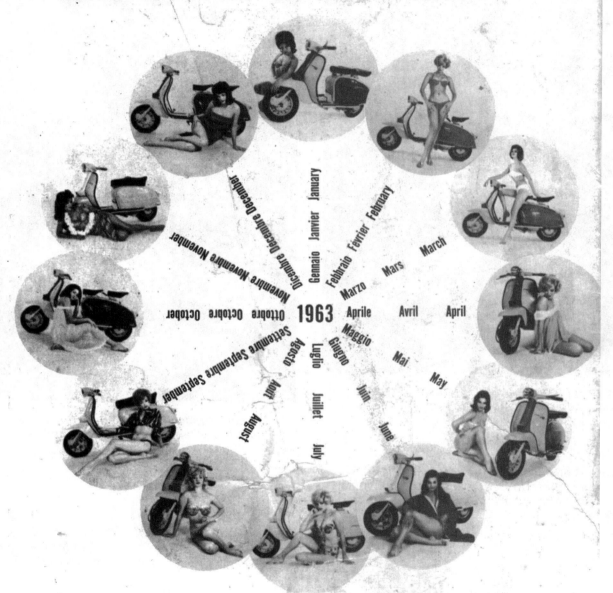

1963 IN LAMBRETTA: ANNO FORTUNATO
EN LAMBRETTA: ANNÉE DE BONHEUR ET DE CHANCE
A LUCKY YEAR FOR LAMBRETTA OWNERS

Queste che vi presentiamo sono le deliziose immagini del calendario Lambretta 1963.

Nous vous présentons les charmantes images du calendrier Lambretta 1963.

Here are some of the wonderful photographs from The 1963 Lambretta Calendar.

Every year they had a colour calendar, and in each December's issue of Notiziario Lambretta *('Lambretta News'), published from the factory, they showed what next year's calendar would be like. Here we see 1963, which was printed in three languages.*

Above *A photograph of Ferdinando Innocenti, who started producing Lambrettas in the late 1940s.*

Below *A business card from Luigi Innocenti which was given to a shop in Italy, along with a book about the factory which I now have in my collection.*

Above *Luigi Innocenti, the son of Ferdinando, took over the Milan works following his father's death.*

COLLECTABLE ITEMS

Parts books

Above right *With every Lambretta model that came out a parts book was supplied for the shops. In the picture you see a selection from 1951–71.*

Handbooks

Right *When you bought a new scooter you got a few basic tools and the all-important handbook, giving you tips on riding and maintenance. The centre book is for a model A. Being in English, and since this model was never imported into England, it was probably for the Australian market, where the A model was imported.*

Left *As models progressed over the years, there were many different repair manuals – the official one from Lambretta, and many approved ones by people such as, R. H. Warring, Sidney F. Page, etc. This is just a selection of the books that were available. In the centre of the photograph is a 'scooter book' in which you recorded mileage, trips, servicing details, etc.*

Below left *From the 'fifties to the 'seventies many scooter magazines were available in Britain, either weekly or monthly. Here are some of them.*

Top right *The Lambretta factory in Milan had its own in-house magazine called* Notiziario Lambretta, *which was sent out to dealers and enthusiasts. It began in 1949 and survived through to the 'sixties, keeping people up to date with articles about about new models, Lambretta club events, and items of general interest. Now it is a very desirable collectors' item.*

Right *As we had our own magazines, so did other countries. Here are some from Holland, France, and Italy.*

Below *In January 1962 the name of* Notiziario Lambretta *was changed to the* Lambretta Club, *still full of news and information about Lambrettas. In Britain we had the* Lambretta Leader, *which was a paper for Lambretta enthusiasts. Also in the picture are two Lambretta diaries of 1959 and 1960.*

Above *These would decorate any wall: a selection of calendars for 1957, 1958, and 1960.*

Left *In this photograph are models that can be bought today, including Cs, LDs, TVs, SXs and GPs.*

Below *'The General' is a plastic kit of an SX 200 which you assembled and painted yourself, but it is more valuable in its kit form. The white model A with rider originated in Italy but was found in England. The three plastic LDs are official Lambretta toys that operated with a friction motor. When they were new they cost 7s 11d (about 40p) but are worth a lot more today.*

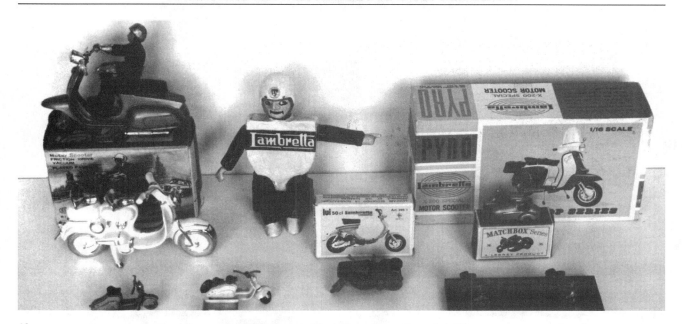

If you were too young to ride a scooter you could always buy a model. There are examples from Denmark, Italy, Spain, Canada, and Great Britain in this photograph.

Britains, a company that still exists today, made an LI 150 with riders. Tri-ang 'Spot on' models are also very collectable. The small models at the front were intended for use with train sets.

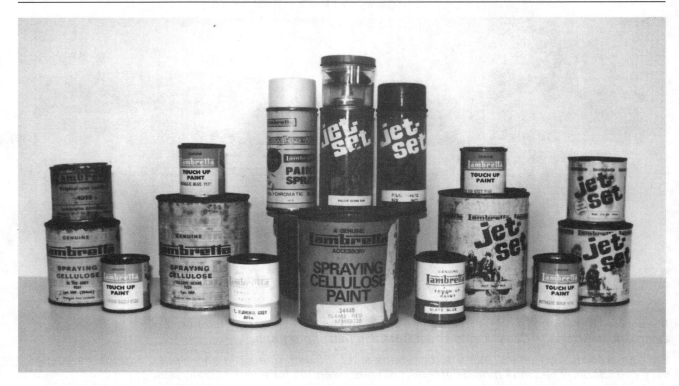

Above *As more colours were added to the Lambretta range you could buy retouching paints in small 1/8 pint cans. Later on spray-cans became available.*

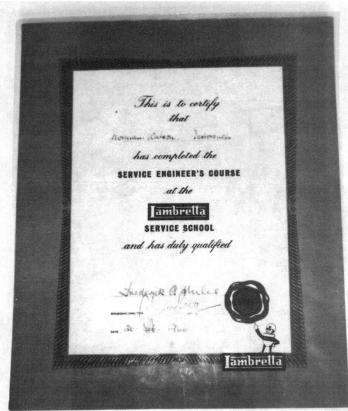

Left *As I mentioned before, dealers had factory-trained mechanics. When you went through the Lambretta training school you were awarded a certificate.*

Publicity

Left *Large blow-up Lambretta beach balls. They came in many colours and were given away at events and rallies.*

Below *Neon was always popular for signs. This example, with 'Lambretta' in red, was made by Brilite Signs of Northampton, who no longer exist.*

Bottom *A blue 'Lambretta Motor Scooter' sign from Brilite and a large 'Lambretta' neon from Italy. The latter was intended for outside use.*

Above *Lambretta's famous logo on a light-up plastic sign.*

Left *The 'Lambretta Agent' light-up sign was made in England. The manufacturer also produced signs for other makes, such as Triumph. The 'Lambretta Innocenti' sign was made in Italy by Brevetta, under the brand name Luxplay.*

Left *As well as glass and plastic, stoved enamel signs were very popular. These came in many sizes and wording.*

Left *A British 'Service Agent' sign to screw onto your wall.*

Below *A smaller version of the 'Service Agent' sign, designed to spin in the wind.*

Left *In Britain this 'Lambretta Man' was a very popular logo, to be found on many leaflets, letterheads, and displays. He is made of stiff card and came in many sizes.*

Above *So that people could see the workings of an engine, cutaways were cleverly produced so that they would still turn over to demonstrate the components in operation. This cutaway is of a model D.*

Left *A Series I frame breather engine mounted in part of a Lambretta frame. These cutaway engines were loaned to the service agents for display and teaching purposes.*

Some of the workshop tools on an official tool board. In this picture there are tools for LDs, LIs and SXs. Most large Lambretta agents would have had a service bay with a tool board, tools, and work-bench.

A tool for holding the engine on the LI range. The left-hand tube goes between the engine mounts with a bar to hold it, and the suspension spring mount fits into the right-hand tube. Then the whole engine could be turned for different jobs.

Left *One of my displays of the different badges that were used on Lambrettas over the years.*

Below *Rear frame and Lambro badges, also LD and D badges. A lot of them are made of plastic, with the background sometimes engraved and painted with gold leaf.*

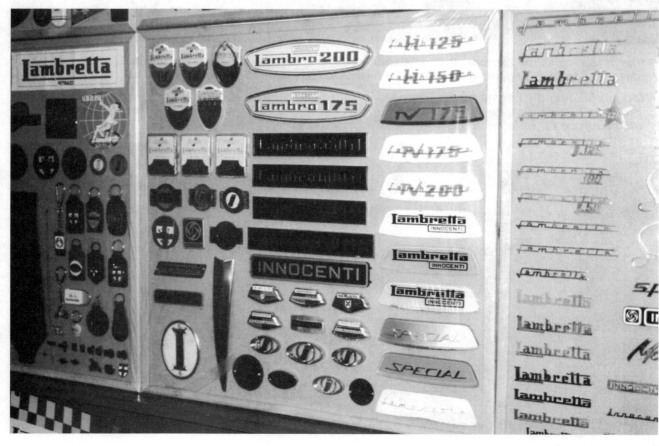

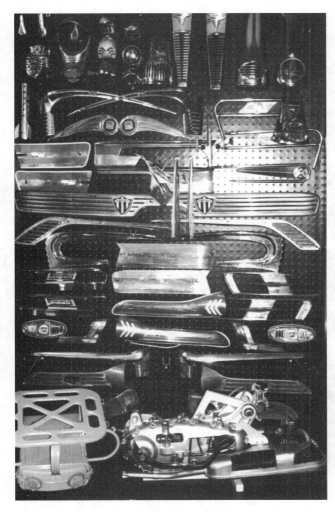

A display of accessories including horn covers, panel trim, and exhaust deflectors.

Mudguard crests, number plate surrounds, and LD air scoops are among some of the most sought-after accessories today.

Ulma was a very big Italian producer of Vespa and Lambretta accessories. In this display are many of their products.

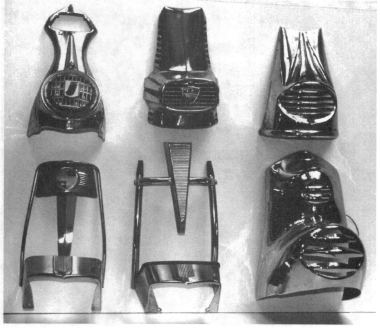

A closer look at some horn casting embellishers covering LI 150 Series I, LI 150 Series II, SXs, and LDs.

Right *Streamers were those once-cheap plastic strips that went into the handlebar ends; but not any more. Today they are very desirable, and hard to find. Ken Cobbing, a name from the past, bought in many parts and accessories from Italy, among them the mud-flaps at right. Also shown are a blue enamel BLOA badge (British Lambretta Owners' Association) and a 'World Lambretta' badge amongst others.*

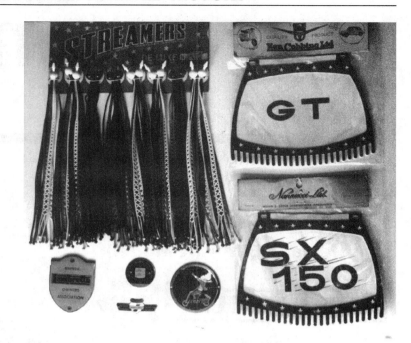

Below *An LD with all the accessories that I can fit on, including a tartan pannier set which was popular in the 'fifties. With all that storage capacity you could do your weekly shopping at Tesco's!*

SPECIFICATIONS

Lambretta 125 M – (A Model)

lambretta 125 m

Made October 1947–October 1948
Total Italian production 9,669
Engine size 125 cc
Bore/Stroke 52 x 58 mm
Carburettor Dellorto MA 16
Gears Three-speed foot change
Horsepower 4.1 hp @ 4,500 rpm
Maximum speed 65–70 kph (40–44 mph)
Tyre size 3.5 x 7 in, front 13 lb, rear 26 lb
Brakes Drums front and rear with steel brake shoes
Tank capacity 6 litres (1.32 gal), 0.8 litres (0.18 gal) reserve
Fuel consumption 39 kpl @ 45–48 kph (110 mpg @ 28–30 mph)
Weight 55 kg (121.25 lb)
Overall length 1,620 mm (64 in)
Overall height 880 mm (35 in)
Overall width 650 mm (26 in) – handlebars
Colours Green, grey, blue, beige, red and maroon
Price 156,000 Lira.

The A model or 125M was the first Lambretta. It was never imported into England, but a few models exist here, imported by private collectors. It was quite something, a 125 cc engine with three speeds and a foot gear-change, which Innocenti only used on this model. In their advertisements they said 'perfect operation and great durability', but anyone who has ever ridden an A will tell you the gears are a little difficult to find, with more than one neutral! It had no suspension on the rear and only a rubber anti-vibration block on the front. The handlebars swept back like those on some motor cycles, and the cables were threaded through with the throttle working on a spiral. This all looked very attractive but it was a nightmare to change cables, especially the clutch. On early models the small 3.5 x 7 in wheels only had three holes, which also held the rim on to the hub, so

that you had to let the tyre down before removing it. The engine was air-cooled, and to get to the points it was only necessary to twist and remove the cover, hence no spanners were required. To get to the engine two bolts were removed in the tool-box and the whole seat tilted up. There were many chrome-plated parts, and with the bright colours of the paintwork it started Lambretta on the road to success.

Lambretta 125 B

lambretta 125 B

Made November 1948–January 1950
Total Italian production 35,014
Engine size 125 cc
Bore/Stroke 52 x 58 mm
Carburettor Dellorto MA 16

Gears Three-speed hand change (teleflex)
Horsepower 4.3 hp @ 4,000 rpm
Maximum speed 65–70 kph (40–44 mph)
Tyre size 3.5 x 8 in, front 14 lb, rear 26 lb
Brakes Drums front and rear with steel brake shoes
Tank capacity 6 litres (1.32 gal), 0.8 litres (0.18 gal)
　reserve
Fuel consumption 300 km (187 miles) per tank
Weight 60 kg (132.28 lb)
Overall length 1,620 mm (64 in)
Overall height 880 mm (35 in)
Overall width 650 mm (26 in) – handlebars
Colours Green, metallic blue, beige and red
Price 170,000 Lira.

After learning from the A model, the B model was
launched. At first glance this looked very similar to the
A model, but the engine had a knuckle-joint on the rear
with spring suspension underneath, and the front forks
were fitted with spring suspension. The cables ran on
the outside of the handlebars, which made them much
easier to change. The gear cable used the teleflex
system, a rigid inner and outer cable which pushed
and pulled to change gear. The size of the wheels had
changed from 3.5 x 7 in to 3.5 x 8, giving a smoother
ride. The linings on the A and B models were riveted
onto the drums and the brake shoes were steel, but
they worked quite well. The frame on these models
was pressed steel, with chrome bars to hold the petrol
tank, seat and tool-box. A few model Bs were imported
and have survived: there is one on display at the
Beaulieu Museum in Hampshire.

Lambretta 125 C (Sports Model)

L̲a̲m̲b̲r̲e̲t̲t̲a̲ 125 c

Made February 1950–November 1951

Total Italian production 87,500
Engine size 125 cc
Bore/Stroke 52 x 58 mm
Carburettor Dellorto MA 16
Gears Three-speed hand change (teleflex)
Horsepower 4.3 hp @ 4,500 rpm
Maximum speed 65–70 kph (40–44 mph)
Tyre size 4 x 8 in, front 12 lb, rear 25 lb
Brakes Finned drums front and rear
Tank capacity 6 litres (1.32 gal), 0.7 litres (0.15 gal)
　reserve
Fuel consumption 50 kpl (141 mpg)
Weight 70 kg (154.32 lb)
Overall length 1,730 mm (67 in)
Overall height 920 mm (36 in)
Overall width 730 mm (28 in) – handlebars
Colours Green, grey, beige and red
Price £125 13s 6d, speedometer an extra £4 4s 0d.

In the early 1950s the C model was launched. This was
the first Lambretta with a tubular steel frame which
other models are based on. The engine was similar to
the B model using the same type of rear suspension.
Instead of using the mudguard to support the front
wheel, they now had separate forks and front springs,
which ran along the outside of the forks. It was very
light with its open frame which made the engine very
easy to work on. The drive from the engine to the rear
wheel on all early Lambrettas was through a drive
shaft with bevel gears to the rear wheel. The tyres
were now increased from 3.5 x 8 in to 4 x 8, which
gave better cornering and a more comfortable ride.
The rear brake was rod operated with a series of rods
and linkages.

Lambretta 125 LC

Made April 1950–November 1951
Total Italian production 42,500
Engine size 125 cc
Bore/Stroke 52 x 58 mm
Carburettor Dellorto MA 16
Gears Three-speed hand change (teleflex)
Horsepower 4.3 hp @ 4,500 rpm
Maximum speed 65–70 kph (40–44 mph)
Tyre size 4 x 8 in, front 12 lb, rear 25 lb
Brakes Finned drums front and rear

Tank capacity 6 litres (1.32 gal), 0.7 litres (0.15 gal) reserve
Fuel consumption 50 kpl (141 mpg)
Weight 80 kg (176.37 lb)
Overall length 1,740 mm (68 in)
Overall height 920 mm (36 in)
Overall width 730 mm (28 in) – handlebars
Colours Green, grey, beige and blue
Price £145 13s 6d, speedometer an extra £4 4s 0d.

As soon as the C model was launched the LC followed, the first to look like a scooter as we now know it. It had leg shields that came up to the handlebars, rear footboards, and side panels that enclosed the engine; on the right-hand panel there was an access flap enabling the rider to turn the petrol on and off, to operate the choke, and to 'tickle' the carburettor for cold starting. The LC was known as the 'enclosed' model because of the panel work, but the engine and running gear was the same as the model C. Instead of the lunch-box on the rear of the C model the LC had a small tool-box under the front seat where spanners could be kept; however, many were fitted with rear racks in order to carry larger items.

Lambretta 125 E

lambretta 125 e

Made April 1953–February 1954
Total Italian production 42,352
Engine size 125 cc
Bore/Stroke 52 x 58 mm
Carburettor Dellorto MU 14 B1
Gears Three-speed hand change (teleflex)
Horsepower 3.8 hp @ 4,500 rpm
Maximum speed 70 kph (44 mph)
Tyre size 4 x 8 in, front 12 lb, rear 25 lb
Brakes Pressed steel drums front and rear
Tank capacity 5.9 litres (1.3 gal), 0.7 litres (0.15 gal) reserve
Fuel consumption 60 kpl (169 mpg)
Weight 58 kg (127.87 lb)
Overall length 1,760 mm (69 in)
Overall height 950 mm (37 in)

Overall width 660 mm (26 in) – handlebars
Colours Green, grey and maroon
Price 108,000 Lira.

The E model was something quite unique because the engine was started by means of a pull-cord along the lines of a lawn-mower. On the early models it had an advance and retard lever to ensure easy starting and to stop it kicking back and injuring the person starting it. The frame was tubular steel in the shape of a letter C, with the upper part being used as its tool-box. The forks were folded back upon themselves and used C-shaped springs with rubbers in between that allowed the fork link to open and close the spring. Because of the model's poor front suspension, many were fitted with a conversion kit which added a spring between the link and the forks. It was brought out as an economy model with a purchase price of 108,000 Lira, only about £43.00 at 1995 exchange rates. Today it is very rare to find a complete E model, as the problems they suffered with the pull-start led to many being converted to the F model kick-start.

Lambretta 125 F

lambretta 125 f

Made March 1954–April 1955
Total Italian production 32,701
Engine size 125 cc

Bore/Stroke 52 x 58 mm
Carburettor Dellorto MU 14 C1
Gears Three-speed hand change (teleflex)
Horsepower 3.8 hp @ 4,500 rpm
Maximum speed 70 kph (44 mph)
Tyre size 4 x 8 in, front 12 lb, rear 25 lb
Brakes Steel drums front and rear
Tank capacity 5.9 litres (1.3 gal), 0.7 litres (0.15 gal)
reserve
Fuel consumption 60 kpl (169 mpg)
Weight 60 kg (132.28 lb)
Overall length 1,760 mm (69 in)
Overall height 950 mm (37 in)
Overall width 660 mm (26 in) – handlebars
Colours Green, grey, brown, blue, off-white and maroon
Price 112,000 Lira.

The F model was basically the same as the E model, but with a kick-start in place of the pull-start. The kick-start went across the front of the engine, and when used in modifications of the E model the leg-shields had to be cut to allow it to go down. The F model had torsion bar rear suspension, an air-cooled engine, and a side-stand, though a bolt-on centre stand was supplied as an extra. As an economy measure it had pressed steel brake drums instead of cast aluminium. Half-way through its production run the F Series II was brought onto the market, which had similar forks to the D model, with a spring-and-rod front suspension. Very few of this model survive today.

Lambretta 125 D – Series I

Made December 1951–January 1953
Total Italian production 69,000
Engine size 125 cc
Bore/Stroke 52 x 58 mm
Carburettor Dellorto MA 18 B2
Gears Three-speed hand change (teleflex)
Horsepower 5 hp @ 4,600 rpm
Maximum speed 70–75 kph (44–47 mph)
Tyre size 4 x 8 in, front 16 lb, rear 25 lb
Brakes Finned drums front and rear
Tank capacity 6 litres (1.32 gal), 0.7 litres (0.15 gal)
reserve
Fuel consumption 50 kpl (141 mpg)
Weight 70 kg (154.32 lb)
Overall length 1,770 mm (70 in)
Overall height 960 mm (38 in)
Overall width 760 mm (29 in) – handlebars
Colours Green, grey and beige
Price 135,000 Lira.

The 125 D was totally different to the C model. It had a tubular frame, without the engine supporting the two halves as in the C model. The engine, being able to move, had torsion bar suspension. This was a tempered steel bar with splines either end which, when loaded, would twist, allowing the engine to pivot. This was used on Lambrettas until 1958. The front forks had springs enclosed in the tube with links pivoting against the springs. As an optional extra

pillion seats and spare-wheel holders could be fitted at an additional cost. These proved popular and were fitted to most scooters. The rear brake was rod-operated with a single teleflex cable for the gears. It had a cast iron cylinder with low wear resistance and an air-cooled aluminium cylinder head.

Lambretta 125 D – Series II

Made April 1953–October 1954
Total Italian production 53,641
Engine size 125 cc
Bore/Stroke 52 x 58 mm
Carburettor Dellorto MA 18 B3
Gears Three-speed hand change (teleflex)
Horsepower 5 hp @ 4,600 rpm
Maximum speed 70–75 kph (44–47 mph)
Tyre size 4 x 8 in, front 16 lb, rear 25 lb
Brakes Finned drums front and rear
Tank capacity 6.3 litres (1.38 gal), 0.7 litres (0.15 gal)
reserve
Fuel consumption 50 kpl (141 mpg)
Weight 70 kg (154.32 lb)
Overall length 1,770 mm (70 in)
Overall height 960 mm (38 in)
Overall width 760 mm (29 in) – handlebars
Colours Green, grey and beige
Price 135,000 Lira.

The Series II D was very similar to the Series I but used a cable rear brake instead of a rod-operated

brake and had different handlebars. It still used the teleflex, and was still air-cooled. Between May 1955 and November 1958 Innocenti brought out the 125 D Series III: only 500 were built, probably for a special order since the 150 D was already in production at this time. The 125 D Series III used two gear cables instead of the single teleflex. Because the D model had an open frame it was popular in Italy, being cooler and more comfortable to ride than the LD.

Lambretta 150 D – Series II

Made October 1954–December 1955
Total Italian production 33,758
Engine size 148 cc
Bore/Stroke 57 x 58 mm
Carburettor Dellorto MA 19 B4
Gears Three-speed hand change
Horsepower 6 hp @ 4,750 rpm
Maximum speed 75–80 kph (47–50 mph)
Tyre size 4 x 8 in, front 16 lb, rear 25 lb
Brakes Finned drums front and rear
Tank capacity 6.3 litres (1.38 gal), 0.7 litres (0.15 gal) reserve
Fuel consumption 50 kpl (141 mpg)
Weight 75 kg (165.34 lb)
Overall length 1,770 mm (70 in)
Overall height 960 mm (38 in)
Overall width 740 mm (29 in) – handlebars
Colours Grey and green
Price £134 4s 1d.

The 150 D had the biggest engine yet. It gave a little more power than the 125, and the gear-change now had two cables instead of the single teleflex. There were cowlings around the cylinder and a fan on the fly wheel for forced air-cooling. There was also torsion bar rear suspension, and internal springs and rods on the front forks. The exhaust had a separate chrome expansion pipe fitted, and there was a narrower tool-box located under the front seat. There was a badge

on the front leg-shields, and pressed aluminium runners to protect the paintwork.

Lambretta 150 D – Series III

Made January 1956–December 1956
Total Italian production 20,835
Engine size 148 cc
Bore/Stroke 57 x 58 mm
Carburettor Dellorto MA 19 B4
Gears Three-speed hand change
Horsepower 6 hp @ 4,750 rpm
Maximum speed 75–80 kph (47–50 mph)
Tyre size 4 x 8 in, front 16 lb, rear 25 lb
Brakes Finned drums front and rear
Tank capacity 6.3 litres (1.38 gal), 0.7 litres (0.15 gal) reserve
Fuel consumption 50 kpl (141 mpg)
Weight 75 kg
Overall length 1,770 mm (70 in)
Overall height 960 mm (38 in)
Overall width 740 mm (29 in) – handlebars
Colours Grey
Price £129 17s 6d.

The Series III 150 model D is the one that was most common in Britain. It was called the 're-introduced' model – basically the same as before with a few changes. The luggage-box lid now had a lock and key. It had a rear shock-absorber on the tail part of the engine and a battery tray for parking lights and the horn. Between the tank and the tool-box was a round rectifier for charging the battery. It was sometimes called the sports model, being much-used in scooter sports trials, etc.

Lambretta 125 LD – Series I

Made December 1951–May 1953
Total Italian production 53,197

Engine size 125 cc
Bore/Stroke 52 x 58 mm
Carburettor Dellorto MA 18 B2
Gears Three-speed hand change (teleflex)
Horsepower 5 hp @ 4,600 rpm
Maximum speed 70–75 kph (44–47 mph)
Tyre size 4 x 8 in, front 16 lb, rear 25 lb
Brakes Finned drums front and rear
Tank capacity 6.3 litres (1.38 gal), 0.7 litres (0.15 gal)
    reserve
Fuel consumption 50 kpl (141 mpg)
Weight 85 kg (187.39 lb)
Overall length 1,770 mm (70 in)
Overall height 960 mm (38 in)
Overall width 740 mm (29 in) – handlebars
Colours Grey and beige
Price 158,000 Lira.

The first LD was an enclosed D model with leg-shield panels and foot-boards for weather protection. It had similar leg-shields to the LC. The right-hand panel had a door to allow access to the carburettor and choke, and for turning the fuel on and off. The panels also had two round portholes with chrome rings. It had a small rear light like the LC, and the petrol filler-cap on the side of the frame. The kick-start was U-shaped to miss the rear foot-boards, and it had a rod operated rear brake. There was an Innocenti badge under the handlebars.

Lambretta 125 LD – Series II

Made June 1953–November 1956
Total Italian production 78,468
Engine size 125 cc
Bore/Stroke 52 x 58 mm
Carburettor Dellorto MA 18 B3
Gears Three-speed hand change (teleflex)
Horsepower 5 hp @ 4,600 rpm
Maximum speed 70–75 kph (44–47 mph)
Tyre size 4 x 8 in, front 16 lb, rear 25 lb
Brakes Finned drums front and rear
Tank capacity 6.3 litres (1.38 gal), 0.7 litres (0.15 gal)
    reserve
Fuel consumption 50 kpl (141 mpg)
Weight 85 kg
Overall length 1,770 mm (70 in)

Overall height 960 mm (38 in)
Overall width 740 mm (29 in) – handlebars
Colours Grey and beige, with optional panels green, blue
    and red
Price 158,000 Lira.

On the Series II LD 125 the leg-shields were changed and the shield badge was inset into them. It was of red and gold coloured plastic, with 'LD' on it. This model had a cable rear brake. Early ones had the flap in the side-panels, but later on the choke and petrol tap were on the top of the main-frame between the seats. Instead of two portholes the panels had a kidney-shaped grill, initially made of white plastic but later changed to chrome steel. The tool tube under the driver's seat was dropped and there was a small tool-box under the right-hand panel instead. Early models had aluminium cowlings for cooling. On some British models there was a luggage-box behind the leg-shields which also housed the speedometer, driven off the rear wheel. The seat covers were brown for the early models and green for the later ones.

Lambretta 125 LD – Series III

Made January 1957–July 1958
Total Italian production 43,635
Engine size 125 cc
Bore/Stroke 52 x 58 mm
Carburettor Dellorto MA 18 B4
Gears Three-speed hand change
Horsepower 5 hp @ 4,600 rpm
Maximum speed 70–75 kph (44–47 mph)
Tyre size 4 x 8 in, front 16 lb, rear 25 lb

Brakes Finned drums front and rear
Tank capacity 6.4 litres (1.4 gal), 0.7 litres (0.15 gal) reserve
Fuel consumption 46 kpl @ 64 kph (130 mpg @ 40 mph)
Weight 88 kg (194 lb)
Overall length 1,770 mm (70 in)
Overall height 960 mm (38 in)
Overall width 740 mm (29 in) – handlebars
Colours Grey and off-white
Price £149 17s 6d.

The Series III LD 125 had a new style of engine with epicyclical kick-start. It was cheaper and less powerful than the 150 model, using a smaller carburettor. Many changes had taken place on the body. The leg-shields were smooth with a chrome 'Lambretta LD125' badge riveted on. The horn and the speedometer were mounted on an aluminium housing on top of the handlebars. On the rear of the scooter was a flat number plate holder, and the rear light was now part of the body. Above the light was a small-tool box with lock and key. From January 1957 to July 1958 Innocenti made 52 LDA electric-start models, probably a special order since Series III LDAs were normally 150 cc.

Lambretta 125 LDA – Series II

Made February 1954–December 1954
Total Italian production 8,694
Engine size 125 cc
Bore/Stroke 52 x 58 mm
Carburettor Dellorto MA 18 B4

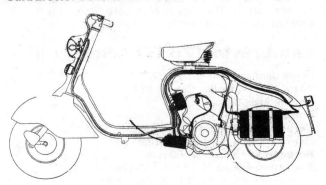

Gears Three-speed hand change (teleflex)
Horsepower 5 hp @ 4,600 rpm
Maximum speed 70–75 kph (44–47 mph)
Tyre size 4 x 8 in, front 16 lb, rear 25 lb
Brakes Finned drums front and rear
Tank capacity 6.3 litres (1.38 gal), 0.7 litres (0.15 gal) reserve
Fuel consumption 50 kpl (141 mpg)
Weight 88 kg (194 lb)
Overall length 1,770 mm (70 in)
Overall height 960 mm (38 in)
Overall width 740 mm (29 in) – handlebars
Colours Grey and beige
Price £150.00 approx.

The electric-start version of the LD was quite something. A six volt battery was incorporated under the left-hand panel. It was about 20 A/H and ran the starter motor, which was fitted to a modified clutch housing, which when engaged drove directly to the clutch bell. There was a rectifier for charging, which changed depending on whether it was night or day. Because it was fitted with a powerful battery the lights and horn ran off it, giving uniform lighting from a low wattage bulb (15/15 watt) at the front and a 1.5 watt at the rear. To start, neutral had to be engaged first, and there was an ivory lever on the handlebars which engaged the starter motor. Once the engine had fired a free-wheel device disengaged the starter motor, to stop it being dragged by the engine and thereby damaging the armature.

Lambretta 150 LD – Series II

Made November 1954–January 1957
Total Italian production 110,186
Engine size 148 cc
Bore/Stroke 57 x 58 mm
Carburettor Dellorto MA 19 B4
Gears Three-speed hand change
Horsepower 6 hp @ 4,750 rpm
Maximum speed 75–80 kph (47–50 mph)
Tyre size 4 x 8 in, front 16 lb, rear 25 lb
Brakes Finned drums front and rear
Tank capacity 6.8 litres (1.49 gal), 0.8 litres (0.18 gal) reserve
Fuel consumption 50 kpl (141 mpg)
Weight 88 kg (194 lb)
Overall length 1,770 mm (70 in)
Overall height 960 mm (38 in)
Overall width 740 mm (29 in) – handlebars
Colours Grey, panel colours green, blue and red
Price £164 15s 2d.

The 150 version of the LD was popular in Britain. It was a little more expensive than the 125 LD but had extra power if a pillion passenger was carried. In the advertising they sold Lambrettas as a cheaper form of car with all-round weather protection. Large screens could be fitted to the handlebars, making it possible to avoid the wind and rain. The 150 had six aluminium runners, rubber inserts, and end caps. On the 125s

they were pressed aluminium. The shield-badge on the leg-shields was blue and white with '150' in gold. The cables came from the controls and had grey rubber sleeving.

Lambretta 150 LDA – Series II

Made September 1955–November 1956
Total Italian production 2,020
Engine size 148 cc
Bore/Stroke 57 x 58 mm
Carburettor Dellorto MA 19 B4
Gears Three-speed hand change
Horsepower 6 hp @ 4,750 rpm
Maximum speed 75–80 kph (47–50 mph)
Tyre size 4 x 8 in, front 16 lb, rear 25 lb
Brakes Finned drums front and rear
Tank capacity 6.8 litres (1.49 gal), 0.8 litres (0.18 gal) reserve
Fuel consumption 50 kpl (141 mpg)
Weight 94 kg (207.23 lb)
Overall length 1,770 mm (70 in)
Overall height 960 mm (38 in)
Overall width 740 mm (29 in) – handlebars
Colours Grey and blue, panel colours green, blue and red
Price £179 17s 6d.

On the second version of the electric-start model the

electrics were changed to 12 volts. This was achieved with two six volt batteries linked together, these being fitted in the rear of the frame with a metal hump to conceal them. The rectifier was mounted under the front seat to help with the cooling, and a redesigned starter motor was fitted under the foot-boards. Some were also fitted with a kick-starter, giving the best of both worlds. As the lights ran directly from the battery they were now very efficient.

Lambretta 150 LD – Series III

Made January 1957–July 1958
Total Italian production 113,853
Engine size 148 cc
Bore/Stroke 57 x 58 mm
Carburettor Dellorto MA 19 B4
Gears Three-speed hand change
Horsepower 6 hp @ 4,600 rpm
Maximum speed 75–80 kph (47–50 mph)
Tyre size 4 x 8 in, front 16 lb, rear 25 lb
Brakes Finned drums front and rear
Tank capacity 7.1 litres (1.56 gal), 0.7 litres (0.15 gal) reserve
Fuel consumption 42 kpl (120 mpg) @ cruising speed of 40 mph
Weight 90 kg (198.41 lb)
Overall length 1,770 mm (70 in)
Overall height 960 mm (38 in)
Overall width 740 mm (29 in) – handlebars
Colours Grey and ivory, panel colours green, blue, red and maroon
Price £159 6s 2d.

By 1957 Lambrettas had really taken off in Britain and sales of the Series III 150 were booming. With its smart two-tone paintwork and quiet exhaust system it was seen everywhere. On this model the carburettor air filter sucked through the frame on an expandable rubber hose, making the engine a lot quieter at high revs. Seat

covers were changed to black, with chrome springs on the driver's seat. The special edition Riviera LDB 150 was available in Britain. This had a 'Riviera' badge, windscreen, rear carrier, spare wheel, saver boarders, heel-plate, and foot-board extensions. It came in grey, American blue, red, and two-tone grey/blue or grey/red. The price was £189 17s 6d, for which sum the purchaser acquired a very special scooter.

Lambretta 150 LDA – Series III

Made April 1957–December 1957
Total Italian production 4,076
Engine size 148 cc
Bore/Stroke 57 x 58 mm
Carburettor Dellorto MA 19 B4
Gears Three-speed hand change
Horsepower 6 hp @ 4,600 rpm
Maximum speed 75–80 kph (47–50 mph)
Tyre size 4 x 8 in, front 16 lb, rear 25 lb
Brakes Finned drums front and rear
Tank capacity 7.1 litres (1.56 gal), 0.7 litres (0.15 gal) reserve
Fuel consumption 39–42 kpl (110–120 mpg) @ cruising speed of 40 mph
Weight 90 kg (198.41 lb)
Overall length 1,770 mm (70 in)
Overall height 960 mm (38 in)
Overall width 740 mm (29 in) – handlebars
Colours Grey, panel colours green, blue and maroon
Price £179 10s 0d.

As with the Series II LDA, this had 12 volt electrics and starter motor, which Lambretta described as 'a long step towards car standards of luxury'. The starter switch was now fitted to the side of the tool-box inside the leg-shields, and the speedo was moved to the top of the handlebars. As an extra a clock and an ammeter could be fitted in the two round holes in the tool-box. Again, a special edition was launched in Britain. Called the Mayfair LDA, it had a passenger seat, rear carrier, spare wheel, saver boarders, heel-plates, foot-board extensions, and a secondary kick-starter in case the batteries failed – all this for £197 14s 8d, making it top of the LD range.

Lambretta LI 125 – Series I

Made June 1958–October 1959
Total Italian production 47,747
Engine size 123 cc
Bore/Stroke 52 x 58 mm
Carburettor Dellorto MA 18 BS5
Gears Four-speed hand change
Horsepower 5.2 hp @ 5,200 rpm
Maximum speed 68–70 kph (42–43 mph)
Tyre size 3.5 x 10 in. front 18 lb, rear 28 lb
Brakes Finned drums front and rear
Tank capacity 8.5 litres (1.87 gal)
Fuel consumption 43 kpl (121 mpg)
Weight 104 kg (229.28 lb)
Overall length 1,825 mm (71.75 in)
Overall height 1,038 mm (40.75 in)
Overall width 710 mm (28 in)
Colours Blue and two-tone grey
Price £155 17s 6d.

The LI range was completely different from the LD, with a shaft-drive bevel gear arrangement. A new body was designed, with a large front mudguard which did not turn with the steering. It still used a tubular steel frame, but now the wheels were increased to 10 in. There was a locking tool-box under the front seat. A steering lock and speedo were standard, with the cables running behind the horn casting. The engine was a new design with a horizontal barrel and four-speed chain drive. Air intake to the carburettor was either through a filter housed between the tank and the tool-box, or via a 'frame breather', which used the tubular frame with the air intake in the grille behind the rear seat.

Lambretta LI 150 – Series I

Made April 1958–October 1959
Total Italian production 110,944
Engine size 148 cc
Bore/Stroke 57 x 58 mm
Carburettor Dellorto MA 19 BS5
Gears Four-speed hand change
Horsepower 6.5 hp @ 5,300 rpm
Maximum speed 78–80 kph (48–50 mph)
Tyre size 3.5 x 10 in, front 18 lb, rear 28 lb
Brakes Finned drums front and rear
Tank capacity 8.7 litres (1.91 gal)
Fuel consumption 42 kpl (120 mpg)
Weight 105 kg (231.48 lb)
Overall length 1,825 mm (71.75 in)
Overall height 1,038 mm (40.75 in)
Overall width 710 mm (28 in)
Colours Blue and grey, panel colours red, blue and green
Price £174 17s 6d.

Horsepower 8.6 hp @ 6,000 rpm
Maximum speed 103 kph (64 mph)
Tyre size 3.5 x 10 in, front 14 lb, rear 21 lb
Brakes Finned drums front and rear
Tank capacity 8.7 litres (1.91 gal)
Fuel consumption 31 kpl (88 mpg)
Weight 115 kg (253.53 lb)
Overall length 1,825 mm (71.75 in)
Overall height 1,070 mm (42 in)
Overall width 710 mm (28 in)
Colours Ivory
Price £199 10s 0d.

The Series I 150 LI was very similar to the 125, but it had a brighter paint scheme than the 125's two-tone grey. On the leg-shields it had six aluminium runners with rubbers and end caps whereas those of the 125 were pressed aluminium. Cables were hidden, but drove directly onto pulley wheels to keep them as straight as possible and ensure a smooth action. The engine was a little more powerful so had a different gear ratio. The back light and rear number-plate now followed the lines of the bodywork. This scooter became known as the 'wide style'.

Lambretta TV 175 – Series I

Made September 1957–October 1959
Total Italian production 18,858
Engine size 170 cc
Bore/Stroke 60 x 60 mm
Carburettor Dellorto MA 23 BS5
Gears Four-speed hand change

The Series I TV was the first of the LI range to be produced, some seven months before the LI. At the time it was something completely new: imagine going from an LD 150, with only three gears and low engine output, to the new TV 175 with four-speed gearbox, capable of 64 mph! However, the engine design was only used on this model, and had its problems. The TV had a central kick-start, with a large spring which was difficult to replace (anyone who has ever had to fit one of these will know what I mean). It had the largest carburettor fitted as standard – even the 200's only went to 22 mm – and had a diaphragm to ensure a smooth flow to the engine. The rear suspension was fitted with a spring and hydraulic shock absorber built in one: this allowed the engine to swivel on silent blocks. Outside wheel edges were chrome-plated. It had a unique exhaust system and 70 mph speedo. The rear light arrangement included a brake light with orange either side of the red centre piece; these are now very rare.

Lambretta LI 125 – Series II

Lambretta **125 li**
seconda serie

Made October 1959–November 1961
Total Italian production 111,087
Engine size 123 cc
Bore/Stroke 52 x 58 mm
Carburettor Dellorto MA 18 BS5
Gears Four-speed hand change
Horsepower 5.2 hp @ 5,200 rpm
Maximum speed 68–70 kph (42–43 mph)
Tyre size 3.5 x 10 in, front 12 lb, rear 18 lb (32 lb with pillion)
Brakes Finned drums front and rear
Tank capacity 8.5 litres (1.87 gal)
Fuel consumption 43 kpl (121 mpg)
Weight 104 kg (229.28 lb)
Overall length 1,825 mm (71.75 in)
Overall height 1,060 mm (41.75 in)
Overall width 710 mm (28 in)
Colours Two-tone grey
Price £157 19s 6d.

Like the Series I, the Series II LI was finished in two-tone grey. The gear-change body and switch-block housing were painted the same colour as the scooter. The main exterior feature was the headlight, which was no longer mounted on the horn casting but was now fitted to the handlebars, so that as you turned the light turned with you. A new-style horn casting was secured with two Allen screws, which held the clip for the new horn casting badge.

Lambretta LI 150 – Series II

Made October 1959–November 1961
Total Italian production 206,020
Engine size 148 cc
Bore/Stroke 57 x 58 mm
Carburettor Dellorto MA 19 BS5
Gears Four-speed hand change
Horsepower 6.5 hp @ 5,300 rpm
Maximum speed 78–80 kph (48–50 mph)
Tyre size 3.5 x 10 in, front 12 lb, rear 18 lb (32 lb with pillion)
Brakes Finned drums front and rear
Tank capacity 8.7 litres (1.91 gal)
Fuel consumption 42 kpl (120 mpg)
Weight 105 kg (253.53 lb)

Overall length 1,825 mm (71.75 in)
Overall height 1,060 mm (41.75 in)
Overall width 710 mm (28 in)
Colours Grey, panel colours blue, green, red, orange, yellow and coffee
Price £169 17s 6d.

There were more Series II LI 150s sold than any other Lambretta. Produced in a range of bright colours, they were exported to every corner of the world. They had two single seats with adjustable spring bases, which with telescopic rear suspension and front trailing links gave a very comfortable ride. As the engine was mounted centrally in the frame this model was very stable even at low speeds. The panels were easily removable to gain access to the engine and carburettor.

Lambretta TV 175 – Series II

Lambretta 175 tv

Made October 1959–November 1961
Total Italian production 34,928
Engine size 175 cc
Bore/Stroke 62 x 58 mm
Carburettor Dellorto MB 23 BS5 (early models) or Dellorto MB 21 BS5 (late models)
Gears Four-speed hand change
Horsepower 8.6 hp @ 6,000 rpm
Maximum speed 90 kph (56 mph)
Tyre size 3.5 x 10 in, front 18 lb, rear 25 lb
Brakes Finned drums front and rear
Tank capacity 8.7 litres (1.91 gal)
Fuel consumption 43 kpl (123 mpg)
Weight 110 kg (242.51 lb)
Overall length 1,830 mm (72 in)
Overall height 1,060 mm (41.75 in)
Overall width 710 mm (28 in)
Colours Pale blue, cream and grey, panel colours blue and red
Price £189 17s 6d.

After the problems with the Series I TV engine, that of the Series II was based on the LI, but with the cc increased to 175 and a different crankshaft, barrel, and piston. To cope with the extra power the front forks were fitted with external shock absorbers and a re-designed back plate and fork links. This model was fitted with a different ratio gearbox, a 70 mph speedo, and a dual seat, and had a brake light on the rear brake pedal. Chrome-plated brass 'Lambretta' and 'TV 175' badges were secured to the panels with nuts, whereas on the LI range they were riveted.

Lambretta LI 150 – 'Rallymaster'

Made May 1961–1962
Total Italian production Built in the UK
Engine size 148 cc
Bore/Stroke 57 x 58 mm
Carburettor Dellorto MA 23 BS5
Gears Four-speed hand change
Horsepower 8.6 hp @ 6,000 rpm
Maximum speed 80–88 kph (50–55 mph)
Tyre size 3.5 x 10 in, 4 x 10 in, front 18 lb, rear 25 lb
Brakes Finned drums front and rear
Tank capacity 8.7 litres (1.91 gal)
Fuel consumption N/A
Weight 118 kg (260.14 lb)
Overall length 1,880 mm (74 in)
Overall height 1,060 mm (41.75 in)
Overall width 710 mm (28 in)
Colours Standard colours with black-striped panels
Price £183 15s 0d.

The 'Rallymaster' was designed by Alan Kimber and built at Lambretta Concessionaires. It was very striking, with distinctive black stripes painted across the side panels. It had a turning front mudguard and a horn casting which aligned with it, originally used on Spanish Series II LI 150s. Built for sporting enthusiasts, it was fitted with many extras including a 4 x 10 in rear tyre, ball-ended levers, perspex sports screen, rally number plates, and a GB plate. There was a handle on the rear for scramble work, and a special instrument panel incorporating a rev counter, stop-watch holder,

illuminated map-board, and a separate switch for the spotlight. The engine was stage two tuned using a large bore carburettor, high performance exhaust, and a special gear ratio.

Lambretta LI 125 – Series III

Made December 1961–November 1967
Total Italian production 146,734
Engine size 123 cc
Bore/Stroke 52 x 58 mm
Carburettor Dellorto SH 18
Gears Four-speed hand change
Horsepower 5.5. hp @ 5,200 rpm
Maximum speed 70–72 kph (43–45 mph)
Tyre size 3.5 x 10 in, front 12 lb, rear 18 lb (32 lb with pillion)

Brakes Finned drums front and rear
Tank capacity 8.5 litres (1.87 gal)
Fuel consumption 48 kpl (135 mpg)
Weight 104 kg
Overall length 1,800 mm (71 in)
Overall height 1,035 mm (41 in)
Overall width 700 mm (27.5 in)
Colours Light grey and light green
Price £134 17s 6d.

The slim style 125 was the start of a long production run. It was a classic 'sixties design which boasted a higher speed and greater fuel economy than the Series II. The bodywork was changed entirely. The front suspension was retained and the rear suspension used the same spring and shock absorber, but about half an inch shorter. Under the panels things were mostly the same as in the Series II, but there was a new carburettor, with a needleless float-chamber for increased mpg. On early models the electrics were four-pole but later they were six-pole. The gear-change and switch block were painted the same colour as the scooter and were normally all one colour.

Lambretta LI 150 – Series III

Made January 1962–May 1967
Total Italian production 143,091
Engine size 148 cc
Bore/Stroke 57 x 58 mm
Carburettor Dellorto SH18
Gears Four-speed hand change
Horsepower 6.6 hp @ 5,300 rpm
Maximum speed 80–82 kph (50–51 mph)
Tyre size 3.5 x 10 in, front 12 lb, rear 18 lb (32 lb with pillion)
Brakes Finned drums front and rear
Tank capacity 8.7 litres (1.91 gal)
Fuel consumption 42 kpl (120 mpg)
Weight 105 kg (253.53 lb)
Overall length 1,800 mm (71 in)
Overall height 1,035 mm (41 in)
Overall width 700 mm (27.5 in)
Colours Blue, red and grey, panel colours blue, red and green
Price £159 17s 6d.

The LI 150 usually had a two-tone paint scheme with the panels and horn casting sprayed the contrasting colour. English models had a battery for parking lights, horn, and brake-light, whilst Italian scooters were direct. The speedo on the Series III was changed from a round shape to the more square shape still used on Indian models today. A lot of LI advertising used Jayne Mansfield sitting or standing on the scooter.

Lambretta TV 175 – Series III

Made March 1962–October 1965
Total Italian production 37,794
Engine size 175 cc
Bore/Stroke 62 x 58 mm
Carburettor Dellorto SH 1/20
Gears Four-speed hand change
Horsepower 8.75 hp @ 5,300 rpm
Maximum speed 91–93 kph (56–58 mph)
Tyre size 3.5 x 10 in, front 12 lb, rear 18 lb (32 lb with pillion)
Brakes Front inlaid disc, rear finned drum
Tank capacity 8.7 litres (1.91 gal)
Fuel consumption 41 kpl (118 mpg)
Weight 110 kg (242.51 lb)
Overall length 1,800 mm (71 in)
Overall height 1,030 mm (40.5 in)
Overall width 700 mm (27.5 in)
Colours Metallic blue, two-tone grey and white, panel colours yellow and red
Price £189 17s 6d.

The TV 175 was a beautiful machine to ride. It was the first scooter with a front disc brake (the disc for which was internal so that it kept clean and dry), and it had extra front shock absorbers for improved damping. The engine was horizontal with a different crankcase to take the larger cylinder assembly, and the silent blocks were now larger to give a smoother ride. A dual seat was fitted,

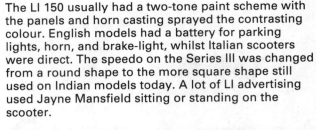

although single ones could be requested. The early model used LI panels, and the contrasting colour was used on the panels, mudguard and horn casting. Later models instead used SX type panels with four flashes on them. The speedo went up to 70 mph and the headlight was the shape of an old threepenny bit.

Lambretta TV 200

Made April 1963–October 1965
Total Italian production 14,982
Engine size 198 cc
Bore/Stroke 66 x 58 mm
Carburettor Dellorto SH 1/20
Gears Four-speed hand change
Horsepower 10.75 hp @ 5,700 rpm
Maximum speed 95–97 kph (58–60 mph)
Tyre size 3.5 x 10 in, front 12 lb, rear 18 lb (32 lb with pillion)
Brakes Front inlaid disc, rear finned drum
Tank capacity 8.6 litres (1.89 gal)
Fuel consumption 41 kpl (118 mpg)
Weight 110 kg (242.51 lb)
Overall length 1,800 mm (71 in)
Overall height 1,030 mm (40.5 in)
Overall width 700 mm (27.5 in)
Colours White, panel colours green, blue, gold, black and red
Price £199 17s 6d.

Many people would say this was the best scooter Lambretta ever produced. Though it only ever had 'TV 200' badges it is often referred to as the 'GT' 200, probably because this was the 'in' word of the day, with Ford having GT Cortinas, etc. This model was built for export only, because something a little faster was wanted in Britain, and not many Italians knew it even existed. It had a front disc brake, fibreglass front mudguard, and used both styles of panels depending upon whether it was an early or late model. It had a very high top gear, which was very good for cruising but made it hard to pull up hills or ride into the wind. The 'TV 200' badge, engraved in white, blue and gold, was fitted behind the seat.

Lambretta LI 150 – Special ('Pacemaker')

Made September 1963–October 1966
Total Italian production 68,829
Engine size 148 cc
Bore/Stroke 57 x 58 mm
Carburettor Dellorto SH 18
Gears Four-speed hand change
Horsepower 8.25 hp @ 5,590 rpm
Maximum speed 85 kph (53 mph)
Tyre size 3.5 x 10 in, front 12 lb, rear 18 lb (32 lb with pillion)
Brakes Finned drums front and rear
Tank capacity 8.5 litres (1.87 gal)
Fuel consumption 38 kpl (107 mpg)
Weight 105 kg (253.53 lb)
Overall length 1,800 mm (71 in)
Overall height 1,030 mm (40.5 in)
Overall width 700 mm (27.5 in)
Colours Green, gold, silver and white, panel colours red and blue
Price £191 11s 3d.

The 'Pacemaker', as it was known in this country (due to the fact that Gerry and the Pacemakers were used in the advertising campaign), can be recognized by the new design side panels, and 'Special' badges on the leg shields and behind the seat. 'LI 150 S' was stamped on the frame and the engine. The latter was a little more powerful than the standard LI, with a close ratio gearbox which was preferred in racing. The 'Pacemaker' badge added in Britain was a gold sticker which fitted at an angle under the 'Special' badge on the front leg-shield. Most 'Pacemakers' were silver, but some that came to Britain – though not many – were 'Golden Specials'. These had badges stating 'Silver' or 'Golden' respectively.

Lambretta SX 125 – Special

Made October 1965–January 1969
Total Italian production 29,841
Engine size 123 cc

Bore/Stroke 52 x 58 mm
Carburettor Dellorto SH 1/20
Gears Four-speed hand change
Horsepower 7.12 hp @ 5,500 rpm
Maximum speed 86 kph (54 mph)
Tyre size 3.5 x 10 in, front 12 lb, rear 18 lb (32 lb with pillion)
Brakes Finned drums front and rear
Tank capacity 8.1 litres (1.78 gal)
Fuel consumption 43 kpl (122 mpg)
Weight 118 kg (260.14 lb)
Overall length 1,800 mm (71 in)
Overall height 1,030 mm (40.5 in)
Overall width 700 mm (27.5 in)
Colours Metallic blue and white
Price 155,000 Lira.

The 125 Special, as it was known, was mostly sold abroad. Only a few were imported into Britain originally, as British riders preferred bigger cc models like the 150 and 200, but over the years many more have come across. With the same bodywork, the Special looked like the SX 150 except that it was painted all in one colour. It was quite fast for its cc, again with special porting and gear ratios. The badge on the front read '125', and not 'X125' as on the 150s and 200s. Most were fitted with a dual seat.

Lambretta SX 150

Made October 1966–January 1969
Total Italian production 31,238
Engine size 148 cc
Bore/Stroke 57 x 58 mm
Carburettor Dellorto SH 1/20
Gears Four-speed hand change
Horsepower 9.38 hp @ 5,600 rpm
Maximum speed 90 kph (56 mph)
Tyre size 3.5 x 10 in, front 12 lb, rear 18 lb (32 lb with pillion)
Brakes Finned drums front and rear
Tank capacity 8.5 litres (1.87 gal)
Fuel consumption 41 kpl (118 mpg)
Weight 120 kg (264.55 lb)
Overall length 1,800 mm (71 in)
Overall height 1,030 mm (40.5 in)
Overall width 700 mm (27.5 in)

Colours Grey and white, panel colours red and blue
Price £184 19s 6d.

Now it was called an SX 150, and Lambretta Concessionaires were quick to pick up the gimmick 'SX appeal', aimed at younger people who were getting into the whole Mod and scooter scene. The SX 150 was the same shape as the 125 Special but had a chrome flash on the front mudguard. Most had two-tone paintwork with a dual seat, and 'X150' and 'Special' badges on the front leg-shields.

Lambretta SX 200

Made January 1966–January 1968
Total Italian production 20,783
Engine size 198 cc
Bore/Stroke 66 x 58 mm
Carburettor Dellorto SH 1/20
Gears Four-speed hand change
Horsepower 11 hp @ 5,500 rpm
Maximum speed 107 kph (66 mph)
Tyre size 3.5 x 10 in, front 12 lb, rear 18 lb (32 lb with pillion)
Brakes Front inlaid disc, rear finned drum
Tank capacity 8.1 litres (1.78 gal)
Fuel consumption 33 kpl (93 mpg)

Weight 123 kg (271.16 lb)
Overall length 1,800 mm (71 in)
Overall height 1,030 mm (40.5 in)
Overall width 700 mm (27.5 in)
Colours White, panel colours red, green, gold, blue, black and purple
Price £219 11s 5d.

The SX 200 had new-style side panels with an 'SX 200' arrow flash. A lot of Italian scooters were all-white with an oxblood seat. It had a front disc and dampers, and a 90 mph speedo. The gear ratio had been changed to that of the 175 TV, which gave a good all-round performance. On the last models the front forks had push-in buffers like the GP, a square horn casting badge, and clip-on side panels instead of handles. The SX 200 is now one of the most sought-after machines.

Lambretta GP 125 (DL 125)

Made January 1969–April 1971
Total Italian production 15,300
Engine size 123 cc
Bore/Stroke 52 x 58 mm
Carburettor Dellorto SH 1/20
Gears Four-speed hand change
Horsepower 7.3 hp @ 6,200 rpm
Maximum speed 85 kph (57 mph)
Tyre size 3.5 x 10 in, front 12 lb, rear 18 lb (32 lb with pillion)
Brakes Finned drums front and rear
Tank capacity 8.1 litres (1.78 gal)
Fuel consumption 40 kpl (112 mpg)
Weight 118 kg (260.14 lb)
Overall length 1,800 mm (71 in)
Overall height 1,012 mm (40 in)
Overall width 680 mm (27 in)
Colours Turquoise and white
Price £184 19s 6d.

The GP or Grand Prix was styled by Bertone, famous for his car designs. It was a contrast to other models, using a black rubber scheme and bright colours for the paintwork. The 125 still had a SH 1/20 carburettor but it used GP 200 gearing, and had a different sprocket set-up. Not too many were imported into Britain at the

time, but a lot have come from Italy recently with DL 125 badging. These were direct models with no battery. The wheels, hubs, stand, and splash plate were painted in silver, with early models still having a grey wiring loom and grey plastic tool-box. On most 125s there was an 'ink spot'. It was said that when the plans were being drawn somebody had dropped ink onto them and that this 'ink spot' was carried through to the final product!

Lambretta GP 150 (DL 150)

Made January 1969–April 1971
Total Italian production 20,048
Engine size 148 cc
Bore/Stroke 57 x 58 mm
Carburettor Dellorto SH 2/22
Gears Four-speed hand change
Horsepower 9.27 hp @ 6,300 rpm
Maximum speed 100–105 kph (62–64 mph)
Tyre size 3.5 x 10 in, front 12 lb, rear 18 lb (32 lb with pillion)
Brakes Finned drums front and rear
Tank capacity 8.1 litres (1.78 gal)
Fuel consumption 29 kpl (82 mpg)
Weight 120 kg (264.55 lb)
Overall length 1,800 mm (71 in)
Overall height 1,012 mm (40 in)
Overall width 680 mm (27 in)
Colours White, orange, red and yellow ochre, panel colours blue and red
Price £212 19s 6d.

GP models had a completely redesigned headset with a new rectangular headlight. (This was not permitted in some countries, such as Holland.) The forks were about 1.5 in shorter than previous models, with shorter leg-shields and a new-shaped front mudguard. All GPs had clip-on panels with a black stripe to give them racing lines. The seat was a very modern shape with angled corners. Under the panels the engine had been beefed-up, and to cope with this extra power a larger carburettor had been fitted, along with a new

crankshaft and fly wheel with thicker tapers. On some models there was a flag transfer on the front right-hand side of the leg-shields.

Lambretta GP 200 (DL 200)

Made January 1969–April 1971
Total Italian production 9,350
Engine size 198 cc
Bore/Stroke 66 x 58 mm
Carburettor Dellorto SH 2/22
Gears Four-speed hand change
Horsepower 11.74 hp @ 6,200 rpm
Maximum speed 100 kph (68 mph)
Tyre size 3.5 x 10 in, front 12 lb, rear 18 lb (32 lb with pillion)
Brakes Inlaid disc brake front, finned drum rear
Tank capacity 8.1 litres (1.78 gal)
Fuel consumption 25 kpl (70 mpg)
Weight 123 kg (271.16 lb)
Overall length 1,800 mm (71 in)
Overall height 1,012 mm (40 in)
Overall width 680 mm (27 in)
Colours White, red and yellow ochre
Price £249 19s 6d.

Sadly this was the last 200 Innocenti ever made. All 200s had a one-colour paint scheme and a disc brake. It was such a good design that Scooters India bought the tooling and are still making them today. GPs were getting into the modern scooter age, with some parts – for example the grille and tool-box – made in plastic to save on production costs. Around June 1970 a GP 200 Electronic was produced. This had Ducati electrics with no points, and in Britain, where it is very much in demand, it had an 'Electronic' sticker on the leg-shields and a special slope-back seat. In Italy the normal GP seat was used. The price for the Electronic in Italy was 211,000 Lira.

Lambretta J50 C-CL-S ('Vega')

Made March 1968–June 1969
Total Italian production 27,812
Engine size 49.8 cc
Bore/Stroke 38 x 44 mm

Carburettor Dellorto SHA 14/12
Gears Three-speed hand change
Horsepower 1.48 hp @ 4,600 rpm
Maximum speed 40 kph (25 mph)
Tyre size 3 x 10 in, front 22 lb, rear 26 lb
Brakes Finned drums front and rear
Tank capacity 6 litres (1.32 gal), 0.8 litres (0.18 gal) reserve
Fuel consumption 62 kpl (176 mpg)
Weight 68.5 kg (151.01 lb)
Overall length 1,700 mm (67 in)
Overall height 1,028 mm (40.5 in)
Overall width 656 mm (26 in)
Colours Orange, red, blue, silver and green
Price 89,500–95,000 Lira.

Most people will recognize this scooter as a 'Vega', though in Italy it was called a 'Lui'. It was very popular there, since the 50 cc engine did not require a number plate – it was like riding a bicycle! Only a couple ever made their way to Britain, customers here preferring the 75 cc models. Again these new step-through models were designed by Bertone, with bright colours and black trim. The basic model had bicycle-type chrome handlebars with different lights. The engine had a completely different casting, much thinner because they only had three gears and the headlights had only main beam, with no dip. They also had a smaller single seat. The suspension was similar to larger Lambrettas.

Lambretta 'Vega' 75 – 'Cometa' 75 SL

Lambretta 75 s
75 sl

Made August 1968–December 1970
Total Italian production 9,402
Engine size 74.4 cc

Bore/Stroke 46.4 x 44 mm
Carburettor Dellorto SH 1/20
Gears Four-speed hand change
Horsepower 5.2 hp @ 6,300 rpm
Maximum speed 82.5 kph (51 mph)
Tyre size 3 x 10 in, front 22 lb, rear 26 lb
Brakes Finned drums front and rear
Tank capacity 6 litres (1.32 gal)
Fuel consumption 55 kpl (157 mpg)
Weight 76 kg (167.55 lb)
Overall length 1,090 mm (67 in)
Overall height 1,028 mm (40.5 in)
Overall width 660 mm (26 in)
Colours Orange, red, silver, green and turquoise
Price £115 19s 6d–£125 19s 6d.

This was the 'Space Age Look For The Year 2000', as Lambretta Concessionaires marketed it. It was a very modern machine, with a 20 mm carburettor, four gears and a top speed of 51 mph. Unlike the smaller 50 cc it had a dual seat and foot pegs and could carry two people comfortably. It had a plastic air filter box which was prone to breaking. (These are now virtually impossible to obtain, as anybody who has tried will tell you.) The 'Cometa' was the only Lambretta with 'oil injection' operating automatically from two separate tanks, with a special pump running off the crankshaft. The Luna line launching, which included the 'Cometa', was on 26 November 1968. With 18 months of detailed planning, over a million leaflets, 20,000 posters, stickers and streamers, it was one of the biggest promotional campaigns ever. Sadly, however, this model was too far ahead of its time, and disappointing sales saw its retail price plummet to £99.

Lambrettino – Moped

Made November 1966–December 1967
Total Italian production 15,677
Engine size 39 cc
Bore/Stroke 40 x 31 mm
Carburettor Dellorto SHA 14/12
Gears Two-speed hand change
Horsepower 1.2 hp @ 4,500 rpm
Maximum speed 39.9 kph (24 mph)
Tyre size 2 x 18 in, front 25 lb, rear 35 lb

Brakes Finned drums front and rear
Tank capacity 2.7 litres (0.59 gal)
Fuel consumption 72 kpl (205 mpg)
Weight 40.7 kg (89.73 lb)
Overall length 1,652 mm (65 in)
Overall height 998 mm (39.33 in)
Overall width 657 mm (26 in)
Colours Orange, red, green, ivory and grey
Price £67 17s 6d.

This was the smallest engine Lambretta produced, and in the face of a strong wind the rider needed to pedal! There was a lot of plastic used, including engine covers, headlight, and petrol tank. The drive to the rear wheel was by chain but was not enclosed as on other Lambrettas, although it had a chain guard. It was fully automatic – simply open the throttle and go! It had spoked wheels with trailing links and rigid suspension at the rear. An exhaust valve lever reduced compression when starting, which was by means of the pedals.

Lambrettino SX – Automatic

Made October 1967–November 1968
Total Italian production 8,922
Engine size 48.46 cc
Bore/Stroke 41.4 x 36 mm
Carburettor Dellorto SHA14/12
Gears Automatic hand change
Horsepower 1.272 hp @ 4,400 rpm
Maximum speed 38.3 kph (24 mph)
Tyre size 2 x 18 in, front 25 lb, rear 35 lb
Brakes Drums front and rear
Tank capacity 2.8 litres (0.61 gal)
Fuel consumption 72 kpl (205 mpg)
Weight 42 kg (92.59 lb)
Overall length 1,652 mm (65 in)
Overall height 998 mm (39.33 in)
Overall width 657 mm (26 in)
Colours Orange, red, green, ivory and grey
Price £69 17s 6d.

The SX Automatic was not an SX 200 but a small

moped, very much like the Lambrettino to look at with plastic trim, spoked wheels, and an air-cooled engine, but now with more power from a 50 cc unit. It had a different exhaust, with two sets of chains going to the rear wheel. It also had a rack for carrying parcels and underneath there was a little tool-box. To ride the SX automatic you used the lever to decompress the engine; once it had fired you just opened the throttle and went. In Italy no speedos or number plates were fitted.

Lambretta 48 Moped – Series I

Made August 1955–December 1957
Total Italian production 34,909
Engine size 47.75 cc
Bore/Stroke 40 x 38 mm
Carburettor Dellorto T5-11S
Gears Two-speed hand change
Horsepower 1.7 hp @ 5,000 rpm
Maximum speed 50–55 kph (31–34 mph)
Tyre size 2 x 22 in, front 21 lb, rear 36 lb
Brakes Drums front and rear
Tank capacity 2.7 litres (0.59 gal)
Fuel consumption 80 kpl (226 mpg)
Weight 44 kg (97 lb)
Overall length 1,900 mm (74.8 in)
Overall height 1,000 mm (39.4 in)
Overall width 620 mm (24.4 in)
Colours Red, blue and grey
Price £71 17s 6d.

This moped was around in the days of the LD. In Britain it was marketed as an auto-cycle, but it was really a moped. The NSU Quickly was very similar, as it was built under licence in Germany. The Ribot, as the 48 was sometimes called, had two speeds – slow, and not so slow! – but it saved a lot of pedalling. It had spring suspension on the front with spring assisted shock absorbers on the back. There was a knob on the right-hand side to disengage the engine, and the pedals were used for starting. If you pedalled backwards it applied the rear brake. Although it only had a small tank it had a range of 120 miles.

Lambretta 48 Moped – Series II

Made January 1959–March 1961
Total Italian production 24,640
Engine size 47.75 cc
Bore/Stroke 40 x 38 mm
Carburettor Dellorto T5-11S
Gears Two-speed hand change
Horsepower 1.7 hp @ 5,000 rpm
Maximum speed 50–55 kph (31–34 mph)
Tyre size 2 x 22 in, front 21 lb, rear 36 lb
Brakes Drums front and rear
Tank capacity 2.7 litres (0.59 gal)
Fuel consumption 80 kpl (226 mpg)
Weight 44 kg (97 lb)
Overall length 1,900 mm (74.8 in)
Overall height 1,000 mm (39.4 in)
Overall width 620 mm (24.4 in)
Colours Red, blue and grey
Price £71 17s 6d.

In the Series II Lambretta 48 the HT coil was moved inside the fly wheel. It was still air-cooled, and had a

handle to facilitate carrying it into the house or into the rear yard to park it. There was a very effective silencer, and the gear change was different, with two cables instead of one. A small tool-box was fitted onto the rack, with a pump on the underside. To stop things getting caught in the rear wheel it had skirt protectors, comprising elastic string fanning out to the rear mudguard. Finally, the stand was a different shape.

Lambretta J 50 – Three-speed

Made October 1964–August 1966
Total Italian production 31,021
Engine size 49.8 cc
Bore/Stroke 38 x 44 mm
Carburettor Dellorto SHB 12
Gears Three-speed hand change
Horsepower 1.7 hp @ 4,500 rpm
Maximum speed 40 kph (25 mph)
Tyre size 2.75 x 9 in, front 21 lb, rear 36 lb
Brakes Finned drums front and rear
Tank capacity 6.2 litres (1.36 gal)
Fuel consumption 63 kpl (178 mpg)
Weight 78 kg (171.96 lb)
Overall length 1,660 mm (65.33 in)
Overall height 1,000 mm (39.33 in)
Overall width 630 mm (24.75 in)
Colours Red, blue, green and white
Price 109,700 Lira.

The J 50 looked very similar to the Cento, but had much less power and was really quite slow. It only used four plastic runners on the foot-boards, with none in the centre. It had smaller 9 inch wheels, which are difficult to find tyres for nowadays. The picture from the sales leaflet shows no rear shock absorber. Italian models did not have a speedo, only a blanking plate. From September 1966 to January 1968 a four-speed version was built, giving better fuel consumption and acceleration, a total of 38,967 being produced.

Lambretta J 50 – De-Luxe

Made January 1968–October 1970
Total Italian production 28,852
Engine size 49.8 cc

Bore/Stroke 38 x 44 mm
Carburettor Dellorto SHB/18-12
Gears Three-speed hand change
Horsepower 1.47 hp @ 4,500 rpm
Maximum speed 38.3 kph (23.5 mph)
Tyre size 3 x 10 in, front 20 lb, rear 28 lb
Brakes Finned drums front and rear
Tank capacity 6.2 litres (1.36 gal)
Fuel consumption 63 kpl (178 mpg)
Weight 80 kg (176.37 lb)
Overall length 1,660 mm (65.33 in)
Overall height 1,000 mm (39.33 in)
Overall width 630 mm (24.75 in)
Colours Red, blue, yellow ochre and green
Price 120,000 Lira.

The De-Luxe was, as its name suggests, an up-market J model. It only had a single seat, but a carrier was fitted behind for packages. The badging on the leg-shield was changed to bolder lettering, with aluminium flashes on the side-panels, similar to the SX 150 with the additional word 'De-Luxe'. On the engine case it had 'DL' as a prefix to the number.

Lambretta J 50 – Special

Made April 1970–May 1971
Total Italian production 13,599
Engine size 49.8 cc
Bore/Stroke 38 x 44 mm
Carburettor Dellorto SHB/18-12
Gears Three-speed hand change
Horsepower 1.47 hp @ 4,500 rpm
Maximum speed 38.3 kph (23.5 mph)
Tyre size 3 x 10 in, front 20 lb, rear 28 lb
Brakes Finned drums front and rear
Tank capacity 6.2 litres (1.36 gal)
Fuel consumption 63 kpl (174 mpg)
Weight 80 kg (176.37 lb)
Overall length 1,660 mm (65.33 in)
Overall height 1,000 mm (39.33 in)
Overall width 630 mm (24.75 in)
Colours Orange, red, green, blue and silver
Price 120,000 Lira.

The 50 cc J range was built a long time after the 125

J, with the J 50 Special being the last model produced. It now had clip-on side-panels with a five-fingered flash and the word 'Special'. There was a redesigned seat like the fast back ones of today, with a plastic handle at the rear (possibly for pushing it!). The tyre size was increased to 300 x 10 in, and instead of runners it had a fitted mat. On the edges of the leg-shield it had aluminium trim instead of the normal rubber beading.

Lambretta 'Cento'

Made March 1964–November 1965
Total Italian production 17,642
Engine size 98 cc
Bore/Stroke 51 x 48 mm
Carburettor Dellorto SHB 18
Gears Three-speed hand change
Horsepower 4.7 hp @ 5,300 rpm
Maximum speed 76 kph (46 mph)
Tyre size 3 x 10 in, front 20 lb, rear 28 lb (35 lb with pillion)
Brakes Finned drums front and rear
Tank capacity 6.2 litres (1.36 gal)
Fuel consumption 53 kpl (151 mpg)
Weight 80 kg (176.37 lb)
Overall length 1,690 mm (66.5 in)
Overall height 1,030 mm (40.5 in)
Overall width 630 mm (24.75 in)
Colours Ivory, light blue and yellow
Price £109 17s 6d.

The 'Cento' was the first of the J range to be produced. It had a light pressed steel frame with a 98 cc engine and three gears. It was aimed at the ladies, only a short prod of the kick-start being needed whilst, being

light, it was also easy to take on and off the stand. The first models had two separate seats, but most had a dual seat fitted. The rear suspension had a helical spring with a separate shock absorber, and there was storage space under the seat for tools and oil. The speedo and headlight were fitted onto the handlebars. All three colours came with grey trim.

Lambretta J 125 – Three-speed

Made September 1964–September 1966
Total Italian production 21,651
Engine size 122.48 cc
Bore/Stroke 57 x 48 mm
Carburettor Dellorto SHB/16
Gears Three-speed hand change
Horsepower 5.8 hp @ 5,300 rpm
Maximum speed 86.7 kph (53.8 mph)
Tyre size 3 x 10 in, front 20 lb, rear 28 lb (35 lb with pillion)
Brakes Finned drums front and rear
Tank capacity 6.2 litres
Fuel consumption 49 kpl (140 mpg)
Weight 90 kg (198.41 lb)
Overall length 1,690 mm (66.5 in)
Overall height 1,020 mm (40.25 in)
Overall width 630 mm (24.75 in)
Colours Light blue, silver, ivory, metallic blue and yellow
Price £139 18s 9d.

The J 125 had the same wide body-shape as the 'Cento'. It was a pressed steel frame with detachable panels and mudguard, but the leg-shields were a fixed part of the frame (as on the Vespa). Early models had two single seats. On the leg-shields they had seven grey plastic runners with matching grey trim.

Lambretta J 125 'Starstream' – Four-Speed (M4)

Made May 1966–April 1969
Total Italian production 16,052
Engine size 122.48 cc
Bore/Stroke 57 x 58 mm
Carburettor Dellorto SHB/16/18
Gears Four-speed hand change
Horsepower 5.8 hp @ 5,300 rpm
Maximum speed 87 kph (55 mph)
Tyre size 3 x 10 in, front 20 lb, rear 28 lb. (35 lb with pillion)
Brakes Finned drums front and rear
Tank capacity 6.2 litres (1.36 gal)
Fuel consumption 49 kpl (140 mpg)
Weight 90 kg (198.41 lb)
Overall length 1,690 mm (66.5 in)
Overall height 1,030 mm (40.5 in)
Overall width 630 mm (24.75 in)
Colours Blue, silver, metallic blue, white and yellow, panel colours blue and red
Price £129 17s 6d, Super Starstream £139 17s 6d.

The four-speed J had a redesigned frame, with a slimmer pair of leg-shields and a new seat mounting that gave rise to a new shape of dual seat, longer and flatter than on other models. The badge on the leg-shields had '125' within a chrome star, with 'Innocenti' in plastic on the horn casting. It had quicker acceleration than the three-speed and boasted 0–100 yards in 8.5 seconds! Later model 'Starstreams' had push-in fork buffers like the GPs, and clip-on side-panels. Included in the 125 M4 production figures were the 'Super Starstreams', of which only a few were built. These had a turning front mudguard that moved with the wheel, and a false horn casting that went down the side of the mudguard. They were produced in two-tone red/white or blue/white paintwork.

Lambretta 125 FB

Made February 1949–March 1950
Total Italian production 2,001
Engine size 125 cc
Bore/Stroke 52 x 58 mm
Carburettor Dellorto MA 16
Gears Three-speed hand change (teleflex)
Horsepower 4.3 hp @ 4,000 rpm
Maximum speed 45 kph (28 mph)
Tyre size 3.5 x 8 in, front 26 lb, rear 28 lb
Brakes Three drum brakes, hand-brake on all three wheels
Tank capacity 6 litres (1.32 gal), 0.8 litres (0.18 gal) reserve
Fuel consumption 39 kpl (109 mpg)
Weight 115 kg (235.53 lb), max 150 kg (330.69 lb)
Overall length 2,460 mm (97 in)
Overall height 1,040 mm (41 in)
Overall width 1,090 mm (43 in)
Colours Metallic blue
Price Not known.

The FB was the first three-wheeled Lambretta produced. (Although there was a picture of an FA in the first A model leaflet, as far as is known none were ever produced). It had the same back end as the B model, but with reduced gearing to carry heavier loads. As this was a cheap, commercial vehicle, instead of the seat-bars and runners being of chrome they were painted the same colour as the bodywork and engine, which was usually metallic blue. Steering was by means of a handlebar with rods and ball-ended joints – not very nice to drive, as it was direct, with no gearing. The brakes operated with cables, the right-hand brake lever working the rear wheel only and the foot-brake working all three. The hand-brake operated on a foot-pedal, locking all three wheels. The brake shoes were steel with the linings riveted onto the drums. There was a choice of front boxes in either wood or aluminium, or it could be purchased chassis-only.

Lambretta 125 FC

Made November 1950–October 1952
Total Italian production 3,001
Engine size 123 cc
Bore/Stroke 52 x 58 mm
Carburettor Dellorto MA 16
Gears Three-speed hand change (teleflex)
Horsepower 4.3 hp @ 4,400 rpm
Maximum speed 45 kph (28 mph)
Tyre size 4 x 8 in, front 22 lb, rear 26 lb
Brakes Three drum brakes, hand-brake and hydraulics on
   rear wheels
Tank capacity 6 litres (1.32 gal), 0.7 litres (0.15 gal)
   reserve
Fuel consumption 35 kpl (98 mpg)
Weight 140 kg (308.64 lb)
Overall length 2,480 mm (97.5 in)
Overall height 1,060 mm (41.75 in)
Overall width 1,200 mm (47 in)
Colours Grey, green and blue
Price Not known.

After the FB came the FC, its rear half being taken from the C model but without the pillion seat. The brakes were hydraulically-operated by a foot-pedal and the battery was moved onto the frame instead of underneath the box, making maintenance easier. The hand-brake worked all three wheels, but was a lever as in a conventional car. Suspension was by means of a pivoting knuckle-joint on the rear, with a transverse leaf spring on the front. Unlike the B and C models the FB and FC were forced air-cooled, with a fan and cowlings. The runners on the FC were made of aluminium and there was a choice of front boxes.

Lambro Lambretta 125 FD – Series I

Made December 1952–December 1953
Total Italian production 4,841
Engine size 123 cc
Bore/Stroke 52 x 58 mm

Carburettor Dellorto MA 18 B2
Gears Three-speed hand change (teleflex)
Horsepower 5 hp @ 4,800 rpm
Maximum speed 55 kph (32 mph)
Tyre size 4 x 8 in, front 21 lb, rear 53 lb
Brakes Three drum brakes, hand-brake and hydraulics on
   rear wheels
Tank capacity 7.5 litres (1.65 gal), 0.7 litres (0.15 gal)
   reserve
Fuel consumption 35 kpl (98 mpg)
Weight 145 kg (319.67 lb)
Overall length 2,510 mm (99 in)
Overall height 1,295 mm (50.5 in)
Overall width 1,300 mm (51 in)
Colours Green and grey
Price Francs 185.

The three wheels of the 125 FD were arranged in conventional tricycle fashion, making it a lot more stable to drive. The front end was similar to a D model, but with stronger front forks and heavier damping. The leg-shields were wider, with six aluminium strips and a hole cut out for the master cylinder which operated the rear wheels. Because the engine was in the middle the drive to the rear wheels was by means of a prop shaft, with two rubber couplings to take up the drive. Between January 1954 and August 1955, 8,280 Series II Lambretta FD 125s were produced, but with few changes. The handlebars had a different teleflex gear change, the light-switch and horn button were changed, a grease nipple was added to the front forks, and there were some minor alterations on the rear brakes. FDs had a choice of open or enclosed rear boxes.

Lambro Lambretta 150 FD – Series II

Made August 1955–December 1956
Total Italian production 9,992
Engine size 148 cc
Bore/Stroke 57 x 58 mm
Carburettor Dellorto MA 19 B4
Gears Three-speed hand change
Horsepower 6 hp @ 4,750 rpm

Maximum speed 60 kph (37 mph)
Tyre size 4 x 8 in, front 21 lb, rear 53 lb
Brakes Three drum brakes, hand-brake and hydraulics on
  rear wheels
Tank capacity 7.5 litres (1.65 gal), 0.7 litres (0.15 gal)
  reserve
Fuel consumption 35 kpl (98 mpg)
Weight 170 kg (374.78 lb)
Overall length 2,510 mm (99 in)
Overall height 1,295 mm (50.5 in)
Overall width 1,300 mm (51 in)
Colours Grey
Price Not known.

After the 125, Innocenti introduced a larger 150 engine.
It had a larger carburettor and a little more bhp.
Instead of the teleflex cable it had two gear-cables. The
spindle and bearings on the front forks were heavier-
duty than the LD, with larger brake shoes. The one-
piece handlebars were chrome, with clamp built on.
Under the seat was the same round tool-box as was
used on model Ds. Rear suspension was by way of
two leaf springs and could carry a load of up to 350 kg
(771.6 lb). Early 150s had the same chassis as the 125
and had three-stud wheels and hubs.

Lambro Lambretta 150 FD – Series III

Made January 1957–June 1959
Total Italian production 6,570
Engine size 148 cc
Bore/Stroke 57 x 58 mm
Carburettor Dellorto MA 19 B4
Gears Three-speed hand change
Horsepower 6 hp @ 4,600 rpm
Maximum speed 55–60 kph (34–37 mph)
Tyre size 4 x 8 in, front 21 lb, rear 53 lb
Brakes Three drum brakes, hand-brake and hydraulics on
  rear wheels
Tank capacity 7.5 litres (1.65 gal), 0.7 litres (0.15 gal)
  reserve
Fuel consumption 31 kpl (87 mpg)
Weight 170 kg (374.78 lb)
Overall length 2,500 mm (98 in)
Overall height 1,360 mm (53 in)
Overall width 1,300 mm (51 in)
Colours Grey
Price £243 12s 1d (chassis only).

Though the last series FD was made in the late 'fifties,
in Britain it continued to be registered into the 'sixties,
as sales were very slow (probably because Britain did
not share Italy's weather). On these later models the
epicyclical kick-start was used. As seen in this scarce
drawing, the tank had a welded seam on the outside
forming a lip, with the HT coil being moved up to a
higher position. All of the wheels had four-stud fixings,
with 10 mm rather than 8 mm studs for greater
strength. Amazingly they had a turning circle of 1.75m!
They had no reverse gear and carried a spare wheel
under the frame. They were very nice to drive and
came with many different boxes on the rear, or as
chassis only for adaptation to suit the owner's
personal requirements.

Lambro Lambretta 150 FDC

Made October 1957–May 1959
Total Italian production 12,118
Engine size 148 cc
Bore/Stroke 57 x 58 mm
Carburettor Dellorto MA 19 B4
Gears Three-speed hand change and reverse
Horsepower 6 hp @ 4,600 rpm
Maximum speed 58–60 kph (36–37 mph)
Tyre size 4 x 8 in, front 28 lb, rear 34–46 lb
Brakes Three drum brakes, hand-brake and hydraulics on
  rear wheels
Tank capacity 11.5 litres (2.53 gal)
Fuel consumption 31 kpl (87 mpg)
Weight 245–275 kg (540.13–606.27 lb)
Overall length 2,570 mm (101 in)
Overall height 1,820 mm (72 in)
Overall width 1,330 mm (52.5 in)
Colours Grey and blue
Price £238 10s 0d.

After the open model FDs, the FDC had an enclosed
cab for the driver. (If doors were required the cost was
an additional £12 10s 6d per pair.) It had scooter
handlebars, with the normal three-speed gear-change
and a pedal to select reverse. To start the scooter a
handle on the right-hand side was pulled, this being

coupled to the engine via a cable. The bench seat, for one or two persons, lifted up to allow access to the engine. Since it would be difficult to give hand signals there were side and rear indicators, and a manually-operated windscreen wiper that was worked by turning a lever from side to side. There were many different boxes available, including an articulated trailer and paraffin drums that fitted directly onto the chassis. Due to their low running costs marketing was also aimed at local councils, for such jobs as road repairs and park maintenance.

Lambro Lambretta FLI 175 – Series I

Made July 1959–July 1960
Total Italian production 10,608
Engine size 175 cc
Bore/Stroke 62 x 58 mm
Carburettor Dellorto MA 19 BS5
Gears Four-speed hand change and reverse
Horsepower 7 hp @ 4,750 rpm
Maximum speed 61 kph (38 mph)
Tyre size 4 x 8 in, front 28 lb, rear 34–46 lb
Brakes Three drum brakes, hand-brake and hydraulics on rear wheels
Tank capacity 11.5 litres (2.53 gal)
Fuel consumption 28 kpl (80 mpg)
Weight 265–287 kg (584.22–632.72 lb)
Overall length 2,590 mm (102.5 in)
Overall height 1,620 mm (63.75 in)
Overall width 1,330 mm (52.5 in)
Colours Grey
Price £269 19s 6d (chassis and cab only).

On the FLI the engine size had been increased to 175 and there were now four forward gears and one reverse. It still kept the same narrow cab and hand-start arrangement as the FDC but the handlebars were those of a Series I LI. There was a friction pad and a knurled screw underneath, which could be tightened in rough driving conditions to stop the steering from wobbling. The electrics were six volt, with an optional

electric wiper motor. The rear light was the same as the D model, with an extra bulb for a brake light. There was a tool-box behind the cab to carry the jack and wheel spanner, while the spare wheel was carried in a cradle at the rear.

Lambro Lambretta FLI 175 – Series II

Made July 1960–August 1965
Total Italian production 71,681
Engine size 175 cc
Bore/Stroke 62 x 58 mm
Carburettor Dellorto MA 19 BS 7
Gears Four-speed hand change and reverse
Horsepower 7 hp @ 4,750 rpm
Maximum speed 61 kph (38 mph)
Tyre size 4 x 8 in, front 28 lb, rear 46 lb
Brakes Three drum brakes, hand-brake and hydraulics on rear wheels
Tank capacity 11.5 litres (2.53 gal)
Fuel consumption 28 kpl (80 mpg)
Weight 290–325 kg (639.33–716.49 lb)
Overall length 2,710 mm (106.5 in)
Overall height 1,620 mm (63.75 in)
Overall width 1,330 mm (52.5 in)
Colours Grey and blue
Price £269 19s 6d (chassis only).

This was the most popular three-wheeler Innocenti made, remaining in production for over five years. It had a redesigned cab which was now the same width as the rear box, and the pull-start was replaced by a kick-start on the left side, with a bevel gear as the engine ran across the cab. On the front of the cab were a larger front mudguard, sidelights, and indicators. On the rear it had a cluster of lights on each side rather than single lights, and a rear window was fitted into the canvas blind. Once again it was supplied both in chassis-only form and with a number of different back boxes.

Lambretta Lambro 200

Made June 1963–July 1965
Total Italian production 18,947
Engine size 198 cc
Bore/Stroke 66 x 58 mm
Carburettor Dellorto SH 1/18
Gears Four speed hand change and reverse
Horsepower 8.9 hp @ 5,000 rpm
Maximum speed 61 kph (38 mph)
Tyre size 4.5 x 10 in, front 28 lb, rear 46 lb
Brakes Three drum brakes, hand-brake and hydraulics on rear wheels
Tank capacity 11.5 litres (2.53 gal)
Fuel consumption 22 kpl (62 mpg)
Weight 348–373 kg (767.2–822.32 lb)
Overall length 2,910 mm (114.5 in)
Overall height 1,670 mm (65.75 in)
Overall width 1,345 mm (53 in)
Colours Grey, blue and green
Price Not known.

The Lambro 200 had the biggest engine that Innocenti used on their three-wheelers. Many things were changed but most importantly the chassis had a main tube running through to the rear, and cross-struts of pressed steel welded on instead of tubes. Tyre size and wheel fittings were increased to 10 in and the front forks were completely redesigned with the links facing forward. It also had dampers to improve road-holding. Inside the cab there was a small dashboard with a speedo and a choke (with a cable some four feet long!). The fuel tank was mounted underneath, and to fill it the cab door had to be opened.

Lambro Lambretta 450

Made October 1965–April 1966
Total Italian production 9,541
Engine size 175 cc
Bore/Stroke 62 x 58 mm
Carburettor Dellorto SH 1/20
Gears Four-speed hand change and reverse
Horsepower 8.45 hp @ 4,800 rpm
Maximum speed 61 kph (38 mph)
Tyre size 4 x 10 in, front 28 lb, rear 46 lb
Brakes Three drum brakes, hand-brake and hydraulics on rear wheels
Tank capacity 11.5 litres (2.53 gal)
Fuel consumption 20 kpl (57 mpg)
Weight 362–382 kg (798.07–842.16 lb)
Overall length 2,885 mm (113.5 in)
Overall height 1,660 mm (65.33 in)
Overall width 1,375 mm (54 in)
Colours Grey and green
Price Not known.

The Lambro 450 is very similar to the 400 with 12 volt electrics, but now it had an alternator capable of 215 W. It had warning lights on the dash, an interior light and electric wipers, and most models were electric start. To cope with all this extra demand the battery was increased to 12 V 18 Alt. The brake reservoir was under the dash, which made it hard to top up.

Lambro Lambretta 550

Made August 1965–December 1967
Total Italian production 34,756
Engine size 198 cc
Bore/Stroke 66 x 58 mm
Carburettor Dellorto SH 1/20
Gears Four-speed hand change and reverse
Horsepower 9.2 hp @ 4,800 rpm
Maximum speed 62 kph (38 mph)
Tyre size 4.5 x 10 in, front 35 lb, rear 53 lb
Brakes Three hydraulic drums and hand-brake on rear wheels
Tank capacity 11.5 litres (2.53 gal)
Fuel consumption 16 kpl (45 mpg)
Weight 375–385 kg (826.73 x 848.77 lb)
Overall length 2,915 mm (114.5 in)

Overall height 1,670 mm (65.75 in)
Overall width 1,380 mm (54.33 in)
Colours Grey, green and blue
Price Not known.

The 550 was the last Lambro in the old styling. It had twin headlights with combined indicators and sidelights, and a new front grille and horn cover, which was detachable and had the badges fitted on. The engine had an alternator which ran from the flywheel on a fan belt; the stator was just a plate with the points attached. It came in two versions, kick-start or electric start utilising a push-button near the ignition switch. Reverse gear was mounted on the left side with a lever; when this was operated and first gear was selected the scooter moved backwards.

Lambro Lambretta 550 N

Made April 1967–March 1969
Total Italian production 13,806
Engine size 198 cc
Bore/Stroke 66 x 58 mm
Carburettor Dellorto SH 1/20
Gears Four-speed hand change and reverse
Horsepower 9.2 hp @ 4,800 rpm

Maximum speed 58 kph (35 mph)
Tyre size 4.5 x 10 in, front 35 lb, rear 53 lb
Brakes Three hydraulic drums, hand-brake on rear wheels
Tank capacity 11.5 litres (2.53 gal)
Fuel consumption 16 kpl (45 mpg)
Weight 390 kg (859.79 lb)
Overall length 2,915 mm (114.5 in)
Overall height 1,670 mm (65.75 in)
Overall width 1,380 mm (54.33 in)
Colours Grey, green and blue
Price Not known.

The 550 N was made in the late 'sixties using the old style body. The engine had been moved back behind the cab, and it had twin headlights fitted on stalks that were round. '550' referred not to the size of the engine but to the weight it could carry. It had opening side windows with electric wipers and still had scooter handlebars. Its very short prop shaft with two rubber doughnuts gave a very smooth ride.

Lambro Lambretta 500 L

Made June 1967–February 1969
Total Italian production 7,758
Engine size 175 cc
Bore/Stroke 62 x 58 mm
Carburettor Dellorto SH 1/20
Gears Four-speed hand change and reverse
Horsepower 8.45 hp @ 4,800 rpm
Maximum speed 61 kph (38 mph)
Tyre size 4.5 x 10 in, front 25 lb, rear 40 lb
Brakes Three drum brakes, hand-brake and hydraulics on rear wheels
Tank capacity 11.5 litres (2.53 gal)
Fuel consumption 20 kpl (56 mpg)
Weight 380–390 kg (837.75–859.79 lb)
Overall length 2,915 mm (114.5 in)
Overall height 1,670 mm (65.75 in)
Overall width 1,380 mm (54.33 in)
Colours Grey, green and blue
Price 455,000 Lira.

The 500 L was different to previous models. The engine was mounted behind the cab and the frame

changed to accommodate it. It had a 175 engine, 12 volt electrics and a dynomotor which acted as a starter and charger. The prop shaft was very short with rubber doughnuts at each end to take up the drive. Externally it differed in having two headlights and a redesigned front grille. In the cab there was a heater which came off the new-shaped head cowling which, when a lever was operated, directed the air upwards.

Lambro Lambretta 550 A

Made February 1968–February 1969
Total Italian production 5,906
Engine size 198 cc
Bore/Stroke 66 x 58 mm
Carburettor Dellorto SH 1/20
Gears Four-speed hand change and reverse
Horsepower 9.2 hp @ 4,800 rpm
Maximum speed 58 kph (35 mph)
Tyre size 4.5 x 10 in, front 35 lb, rear 53 lb
Brakes Three hydraulic drums, hand-brake on rear wheels
Tank capacity 11.5 litres (2.53 gal)
Fuel consumption 16 kpl (45 mpg)
Weight 385 kg (848.77 lb)
Overall length 3,225 mm (127 in)
Overall height 1,670 mm (65.75 in)
Overall width 1,480 mm (58 in)
Colours Grey, green and blue
Price 455,000 Lira.

The 550 A was a similar style to the other twin headlight Lambros, except that the engine had been moved back onto the chassis behind the cab. To gain access the back box could be tilted, allowing work to be carried out on the carburettor and filters, etc. The chassis was made of pressed steel punched with holes to lighten it. The rear mudguards were attached to the chassis so that the rear box was free to move. It had a payload of 550 kg, and to cope with this had twin leaf springs and hydraulic shock absorbers on the rear.

Lambro Lambretta 550 V

Made February 1969–December 1969
Total Italian production 8,166

Engine size 198 cc
Bore/Stroke 66 x 58 mm
Carburettor Dellorto SH 2/22
Gears Four-speed hand change and reverse
Horsepower 10 hp @ 4,800 rpm
Maximum speed 64 kph (40 mph)
Tyre size 4.5 x 10 in, front 35 lb, rear 53 lb
Brakes Three hydraulic drums, hand-brake on rear wheels
Tank capacity 10 litres (2.2 gal)
Fuel consumption 21 kpl (60 mpg)
Weight 390 kg (859.79 lb)
Overall length 3,480 (137 in)
Overall height 1,635 mm (64.33 in)
Overall width 1,510 mm (59.5 in)
Colours Grey, green and blue
Price Not known.

The 550 V had a rear-mounted engine with a dynostart to start and charge the engine. The heater ran via a large diameter hose from the head cowling to the cab, where it could be regulated with a lever. The inside was black, with the option of handlebars or a steering wheel, and the pedals were on the floor. There was an oblong speedo, and the wipers were electric and incorporated a windscreen washer. As the engine had been moved out of the cab the tools and jack were stowed underneath the driver's seat.

Lambretta Lambro 550 M

Made March 1969–December 1969
Total Italian production 2,591
Engine size 198 cc
Bore/Stroke 66 x 58 mm
Carburettor Dellorto SH 2/22
Gears Four-speed hand change and reverse
Horsepower 10 hp @ 4,800 rpm
Maximum speed 64 kph (40 mph)
Tyre size 4.5 x 10 in, front 35 lb, rear 53 lb
Brakes Three hydraulic drums, hand-brake on rear wheels
Tank capacity 10 litres (2.2 gal)
Fuel consumption 21 kpl (60 mpg)
Weight 390 kg (859.79 lb)
Overall length 3,480 mm (137 in)

Overall height 1,635 mm (64.33 in)
Overall width 1,510 mm (59.5 in)
Colours Grey, green, yellow and orange
Price Not known.

The square-shaped Lambro range ran through 1967–72. They were all very similar to look at, with only small differences. The 550 M had a chrome grille on the front mudguard, square lights set into two pods, a driver's wing mirror, and an electric starter. Like the 550 V it came with either handlebars or a steering wheel – offset to one side so that a passenger could be carried – with reduction gears for lighter turning and parking. Where it had a steering wheel it also had a foot-operated clutch and brake pedal like a car. The boxes on the rear had reversed panel indentations and mudguards, half steel and half plastic. A 550 ML was produced from March 1970 to July 1971 and took over from the 550 M, 1,654 being made. This looked the same as the 550 M but came with 175 and 200 cc engines and had small changes to gear linkages, etc.

Lambro Lambretta 500 ML – 175 cc and 200 cc

Made September 1969–September 1971
Total Italian production 4,828
Engine size 175 cc and 200 cc – two versions
Bore/Stroke 62 x 58 mm and 66 x 58 mm
Carburettor Dellorto SH 2/22
Gears Four-speed hand change and reverse
Horsepower 10 hp @ 4,800 rpm
Maximum speed 64 kph (40 mph)
Tyre size 4.5 x 10 in, front 35 lb, rear 53 lb
Brakes Three hydraulic drums, hand-brakes on rear
wheels
Tank capacity 10 litres (2.2 gal)
Fuel consumption 21 kpl (60 mpg)
Weight 370 kg (815.7 lb)
Overall length 3,020 mm (119 in)
Overall height 2,050 mm (81 in)
Overall width 1,635 mm (64.33 in)
Colours Grey, green, yellow and orange
Price Not known.

The 500 ML, which came in two engine sizes, was completely different from the previous models, with a much squarer shape, better fitting doors, and a general car-like finish. The trim was black, with black plastic rear mudguards, black seats, mats, dashboard, and grips. The front suspension was beefed-up, with trailing links and shock absorbers and springs together. The wheels had cast hubs. The engine was moved outside the cab to cut down on noise and smell. As with the 550 V and 550 M, the 500 ML could have a steering wheel instead of the normal handlebars.

Lambro Lambretta 600 M

Made January 1970–November 1971
Total Italian production 5,128
Engine size 198 cc
Bore/Stroke 66 x 58 mm
Carburettor Dellorto SH 2/22
Gears Four-speed hand change and reverse
Horsepower 9.8 hp @ 4,800 rpm
Maximum speed 62.3 kph (38 mph)
Tyre size 4.5 x 10 in, front 35 lb, rear 53 lb
Brakes Three hydraulic drums, hand-brake on rear
wheels
Tank capacity 10 litres (2.2 litres)
Fuel consumption 18.5 kpl (52 mpg)
Weight 390 kg (859.79 lb)
Overall length 3,480 mm (137 in)
Overall height 1,635 mm (64.5 in)
Overall width 1,510 mm (59.5 in)
Colours Grey, green, blue and orange
Price Not known.

The 600 range could carry loads weighing 600 kg. The 600 M had scooter handlebars (this was very popular, as not everybody liked driving a car) but no front brake-lever, since the floor pedal worked the brakes on all three wheels. It had twin square headlights with separate sidelights and indicators, and a chrome front grille with a GP style 'i' badge on the front. The back box could tip to allow access to the engine and gearbox.

Lambretta Lambro 600 V

Made January 1970–January 1972
Total Italian production 11,326
Engine size 198 cc
Bore/Stroke 66 x 58 mm
Carburettor Dellorto SH 2/22
Gears Four-speed hand change and reverse gear
Horsepower 9.8 hp @ 4,800 rpm
Maximum speed 62.3 kph (38 mph)
Tyre size 4.5 x 10 in, front 35 lb, rear 53 lb
Brakes Three foot-operated hydraulic drums, hand-brake on rear wheels
Tank capacity 10 litres (2.2 gal)

Fuel consumption 18.5 kpl (52 mpg)
Weight 390 kg (859.79 lb)
Overall length 3,480 mm (137 in)
Overall height 1,635 mm (64.5 in)
Overall width 1,510 mm (59.5 in)
Colours Green, orange, grey and blue
Price Not known.

The 600 V was the same as the 600 M but with a car steering wheel, offset to allow a passenger to sit alongside. The doors had opening quarter lights with a wing mirror for the driver. There was an interior light and heater control. The carburettor was rubber-mounted, between two rubber hoses, one to the air filter and the other one to the manifold. There were jacking points front and rear to allow the wheels to be changed, and heavy duty rear springs were used with extra hydraulic damping. Sadly this was the last machine to come off the production line from Innocenti after 25 years. The tooling for this model was sold off to Scooters India and it is still being produced today.

CONCLUSION

For people who once owned one, the name of Lambretta is a reminder of the past. Even Ferdinando Innocenti would never have guessed that today, some 49 years after the first model A came off the production line, they would still be so popular. Of the millions that were sold many are still to be found world-wide, either with their original owners or with collectors such as myself. For many of us they represent a large part of our lives, and we get tremendous pleasure from owning one. Speaking for myself, it takes me back to 1967, the days of warm weather, 'sixties music, mod clothes, and, of course, Lambrettas. What makes people fall in love with the Lambretta is hard to say, but once bitten by the bug it is very hard to shake it off. The Innocenti factory in Milan closed down completely two years ago, and where Lambrettas were once parked dead leaves blow in the wind; there is a rumour that a huge shopping centre will be built on the site. Nobody really knows why Innocenti decided to stop producing scooters. However, scooter sales were declining, while Innocenti car sales were increasing, and there were industrial disputes in the factory. Unfortunately, with all these things going on, Innocenti ceased production in 1972. The tooling for the GP range went to India, where – as mentioned earlier – they are still being made today: how long for is anybody's guess, but they can never replace the original Italian Lambrettas.

When you look at the GP today it is hard to believe it was styled some 28 years ago, and you can't help wondering whether, if Innocenti was still producing scooters, we would today have had a twin cylinder, or a four stroke, or even a scooter that would do 100 mph? In Britain the two-wheel market remains depressed, but in Italy you still see scooters everywhere – mostly Vespas, sad to say, but occasionally the odd Lambretta. Fortunately many people share my love for Lambrettas, and it is this that has made collecting scooters and memorabilia so enjoyable. I hope that people reading this book will find it interesting and informative, and share with me the wish that Lambrettas carry on forever! There are still many Lambrettas, parts, and memorabilia out there somewhere, so keep looking!